"Gold breaks seven hundred dollar level!"

Noted economist says: "Gold is money; paper is nothing but a promise..."

"Gold rises as dollar drops—decades of inflation and upheaval prophesied..."

"In the coming days of currency collapse and social anarchy, the only survivors may be those who have studied and learned from this book..."

"This book may save your life!!!"

THE SMALL INVESTOR'S GUIDE TO GOLD

DR. ISRAEL BECKHARDT

MANOR
BOOKS
INC.

First Printing 1975
Second Printing 1980

Manor Books Inc.
45 East 30th Street
New York, N.Y. 10016

ISBN: 0-532-23232-1

For my wife, Minca,
from whose experience
I learned much.

CONTENTS

About the author

From his personal acquaintance with many people, including his wife, whose lives were saved by gold during the wild inflations in Europe after World War II, Dr. Beckhardt learned much that can be of use to us in these troubled times.

As a lawyer of forty-three years standing, Dr. Beckhardt has specialized in corporation litigation and manages his own investments. He believes "gold is the only insurance policy you can buy."

INTRODUCTION

Gold.

It's more than just a metal. More than just a word.

It's a dream—of wealth, happiness...that magical, elusive phantasm sought by alchemists of old...the source of endless maniacal pleasure...the bait that drew plundering Spanish conquerors across uncharted oceans in search of the golden city—Eldorado...the catalyst that propelled thousands of dreamers to California in 1848, to the outer reaches of the cold, Arctic Yukon in the 1890's...

....and which—even today—remains the essence of material success.

The price of gold reflects fiscal and government instability, global unrest, inflation, war and depression. It is the ultimate store of value when traditional investments are overrun by uncertainty. The skyrocketing price of gold is an indictment of previous world economic policies.

It's been five years since *The Small Investor's Guide to Gold,* by Dr. Israel Beckhardt, was first published. At that time, gold was selling for the then unheard of price of $150 an ounce. As of the second printing of this book, gold has exploded to over $700 an ounce.

The main reason for this astronomical rise in price is due to one of several forces Dr. Beckhardt warned of in 1975—namely, the emergence of the Oil Producing and Exporting Countries as a major political/economic force.

Due to the insatiable demand for cheap crude by the superpowers, the disjointed third world nations, rather than take sides, have united to take their place in the world arena as formidable contenders.

The fuel for the skyrocketing rise in gold prices was due in part to the United States' Treasury Department printing dollars of little value.

By regulating prices of oil, we forced American oil companies to export our technology. We addicted ourselves to superhighways, oversized cars, all the while deluded by cheap energy. the 1973 oil embargo was the beginning of oil politics whose price was tolerated by deficit spending.

This oil was paid for *not* with products and

services—but by printing presses. The nomads we made kings have sent their princes to western schools to learn our economics. Upon returning to sit at the right hand of their fathers they bore the all-important news—that the U.s. is in the printing business. In short, we were stealing their oil.

As a result, Old World beliefs and New World economic theories have come to our rescue. OPEC nations now accept a basket of currencies for payment of their goods. These are the German Deutschmark, the Swiss Franc, and the pound sterling (countries whose economies function independent of the price of oil and produce a healthy balance of trade). In addition, the "basket" will require some percentage of silver and gold to establish a basis value.

In effect, the world is returning to a precious metal standard—via OPEC fiat.

In the past, the price of gold was measured by its relationship to such ubiquitous commodities as wheat or grain. Currently, energy is a most demanded commodity, and the suppliers will barter commodities they need; all in relationship to gold.

The banking system developed by the Medici's of Italy hinged on two premises:

1. Not everyone will run to the bank for their

savings at the same time. By setting up a small reserve the bank can lend out exponential amounts of dollars, providing:

2. The banking system is a "closed" banking system.

When money was privately minted, this system worked well. Deficit financing has bastardized the system by demands put upon those who mint the money.

By pumping money into the system that is not backed by goods and services, the existing money is made less valuable. This folly, legitimitized by Keynesian economics, has run its course. The phoenix of a new economics is emerging as the purchase of gold draws money out of circulation and its intrinsic value will increase as the printing presses work overtime.

Over the past four decades governments have clouded monetary and fiscal policy behind a veil of secrecy. But now, consumers can vote in areas beyond the manipulation of government self-propogation.

Gold is truly the currency of the masses.

Specifically, an investor can make money in good and bad times, *if* the portfolio is well balanced.

When the economy is healthy, traditional investments (with heavy emphasis on strategic economic sectors) will ride the cresting wave of prosperity. When the economy ebbs (which is a normal event in the economic cycle) a defensive portfolio can weather the setback.

Regardless of the theme behind your portfolio, it's a good idea to maintain 10% of your gross net worth in physical gold.

Timing is a sixth sense that separates the professional investor from the amateur. The pro tends to have an acute sense of timing. If you can participate in 60% of the price movement of your investment, consider yourself a successful investor.

Catastrophe, however, surprises even the most astute investor. Gold will prove the most valuable asset. Since gold is a reserve against crisis, it would be unwise to be totally invested in gold unless a crisis exists.

Gold can be owned in many forms, the combinations of which are creatively discussed and brought to light through the personal experiences of Dr. Beckhardt.

It's never too late to add more gold to your portfolio. It wasn't long ago that people were saying that at $300 an ounce it was too high—and then again at $400—and $500—and $600—and $700! But in the long run, gold is still over $600, and John Meynard Keynes is dead.

The optimum method for accumulating the recommended 10% of your gross value in gold is "dollar cost average". This is a system in which you discipline yourself to buying x dollars worth of gold (regardless of the current market price), as opposed to x ounces of gold (regardless of the current market price). Dollar cost averaging works best while systematically buying in an upward trending market that has normal up and down price fluctuations. Unit cost averaging out performs DCA when the price runs up with few price setbacks.

Gold has taken on new importance in the 1980's.

The price has risen because of the demands put on it by economic laws respected by our forefathers when *they* were nomads and jewelry and gems were the only true store of wealth. The times have changed, but man's concerns remains the same...gold is a simple measure of fear and greed—and as long as man is run by these tenets, the price of gold will always rise, whether in the trading pits or the minds of men.

Gold ownership has been propagandized as a most unAmerican investment, as its purchase saps money from the economic system.

This theory may prove to be as counterfeit as the Free Lunch philosophy.

Chapter I

The Intention of This Book

The American people is about to be given a choice which has not been available for more than 40 years. As this is written, on August 14, 1974, President Ford signed into law a bill lifting the prohibition on gold ownership by United States citizens which has been in effect since February, 1934. On January 1, 1975, private citizens will once more be free to buy, sell and own gold in any form including bullion. Several New York Stock Exchange member firms have already announced that they have obtained exchange approval to sell gold in small-sized bars.

Among those planning to deal in gold bullion are Merrill, Lynch, Pierce, Fenner and Smith, Inc., Bache & Co., Inc. and Paine, Webber, Jackson & Curtis, Inc. Merrill Lynch & Co. the parent of the brokerage concern, which has 262 offices around the world, is joining up with Handy &

Harman, the metals dealer and fabricator, and Samuel Montagu & Co. of London, a leading wholesale gold dealer to operate a firm to be known as Merrill Lynch, Montagu, Handy & Harman.

Other indications of the mounting interest in gold trading are recent announcements that the American Stock Exchange and many commodity exchanges are readying plans for trading gold contracts. At the retail level, Alexander's, Inc. and May Department Stores Company, Inc. are preparing to deal in gold.

Merrill Lynch says it will offer gold in half and one ounce wafers and in bars of 5, 10, 50, 100 and 400 ounces and also in one kilogram (about 32 ounces) size. It says it would store the gold free for six months and at a small charge after that.

Whenever one has a choice, he is required to take action. It must be recognized that even failure to take action is the making of a choice. In order to make an intelligent choice it is necessary to have information from which to draw conclusions and make a judgment. It is the intention of this book to provide some background for the ordinary citizen who has never considered whether he should buy gold or not to come to some conclusion.

Foretelling the future is always difficult if not impossible. What will happen after the ban on the purchase of gold is removed, has given rise to conflicting opinions. Some experts think that there is a pent-up demand which will result in a burst of buying, at least at first, and then taper off. Others think that the situation will be more like what happened in Japan which allowed its citizens to begin owning gold in April, 1973. While substantial amounts of gold were bought, there was no great rush to hoard.

The most likely expectation is that in the long run the demand by Americans to use their new found freedom to buy gold will be determined by what happens on the inflation front and will chiefly depend on what happens to confidence in the existing currency.

It is not the intention of this book to make an exhaustive study of all of the factors entering into the question of owning gold but rather to provide a guide to what considerations should enter into such a decision. And if the decision is made to buy gold then how to do it.

The question is an urgent one because of the increasing rate of inflation from which we are all suffering. This inflation has an impact upon all of us as we see the daily increases in the prices of almost everything that we buy and especially when we have a concomitant realization of how the value of cash, bank accounts, and bonds is melting away.

What we are witnessing is a new experience for almost all living Americans. While there have been periods of disastrous inflation in past American history, none alive today have experienced anything such as is now taking place. Even more importantly, this inflation seems to be world-wide, affecting all currencies, especially in the free world and no one seems to have any reasonably certain means for controlling it.

The newspapers of September 13, 1974, disclosed that the Labor Department's Bureau of Labor Statistics reported that wholesale prices rose 3.9% in August, 1974 for a total of 17.81% in the preceding 12 months. This was the third largest increase in the 35 years that the index has been published and came to 167.4 per cent of its 1967 base. The Consumer Price Index rose 1.3% in August 1974—an annual rate of 15.6%. This brought the Consumer Price Index to 150.2% of the 1967 average. This was a sharp blow to the administration economists who had hoped inflation would begin abating.

Earlier *The Wall Street Journal* of June 24, 1974 in a weekly column, "The Outlook", carried a very pessimistic analysis of the possibility of controlling this rampant inflation. The column begins "All those hopeful predictions from the White House forecasting a significant easing of the rate of inflation by the end of this year mask a deep foreboding. Top government officials are worried that their inflation forecast again may be rendered inoperative. This time, the sinister force is likely to be one that the Nixon administration is especially unequipped to cope with—a wage explosion."

The column closes on the following happy note: "Discouraged administration insiders admit they have no answers. 'All I can see,' laments one, 'is more inflation than has been forecast.' "

More recently, *The Kiplinger Washington Letter*, which has been providing news and advice to businessmen for more than 50 years, in its issue of October 11, 1974, said, "Obviously Ford's economic package is going to bog down badly. Congress is in no hurry, probably will do nothing big until next year. So you can expect inflation to continue roaring on for months to come."

What can the man in the street do to protect himself from this ominous prospect? It is to that question that this book is addressed.

Chapter II

Some Notes from Personal Experience

Minca and I were married in 1960. She is a native of Romania. When she was born Romania was a monarchy which conducted the government in the traditions and atmosphere of the 18th century. In the 30's this government was supplanted by the fascistic regime of the Iron Guard which when World War II broke out carried Romania into the conflict on the side of Germany. The Nazis came into the country in force but allowed the indigenous government to remain in nominal control, much like the situation which prevailed in Italy and Vichy France. After the defeat of the Nazis, Russian, British and American forces occupied the country but after a few months the Americans and British withdrew, allowing the Russians to install a Communist regime which remains in power to this day. In 1950 Minca managed to escape to Israel which was experiencing a period of extreme scarcity and austerity after its victorious War of Independence of 1948.

In Romania, during and after the war, Minca experienced what it is like to live through a hyperinflation. She saw the value of the currency diminish at a rapid rate. Goods which cost one lei rose to 100 lei, then 1000 lei and hundreds of thousands of lei. When she arrived in Israel, the Israeli pound was worth almost $5. When she came with me to the U.S. in 1960, the Israeli pound was worth about 50 cents. Now it is worth less than 17 cents.

It was this experience with the ravages of inflation which accounted for an attitude which I observed in Minca that was strange to me at the time. I noticed that Minca had very little in savings in cash or in the bank but that she did have a rather extensive collection of gold bracelets and gold coins. She explained to me that her experience of what it was like to have gone through two inflationary experiences, resulted in her having confidence only in the tangible possession of gold and gold objects. She told me many stories about people whose lives had been saved because of the possession of gold and jewelry.

After we were married, I observed that she seemed to carry this attitude forward even after coming to the United States, so that she had what appeared to me to be a mania for the acquisition of gold. Whenever we travelled she would pick up gold bracelets and chains. She tried to tell me that this was not because of any obsessive interest in jewelry, but that she regarded these possessions as ultimate investments in the event of serious political or economic trouble. I also observed that when she bought these gold items she did not buy them purely on the basis of whether she liked the object or not, but she would always ask the jeweler to give her, in writing, the specific gold content of what she bought and she always made sure not to pay too much for the "work," but rather to buy only when the price was not excessively above the value of the gold in the item.

At that time, in the early 60's, I smiled rather indulgently at these practices, feeling that they were based on far-fetched fears which I insisted were completely irrelevant to life in America.

I particularly recall a specific occurrence which, in the light of hindsight, has taken on a great deal of significance. As I recall it, we were on a long drive in our car in the spring of 1961 or 1962. The radio was turned on and the program developed into an interview with the economic writer, Eliot Janeway. During the interview Mr. Janeway pointed out that many years had passed since that day in February 1934 when the value of the dollar had been fixed by pricing gold at $35 an ounce. He traced the decline in the purchasing value of the dollar in the years immediately preceding the interview and made a strong argument that the dollar, even then, should be devalued by a substantial increase in the price of gold.

Mr. Janeway developed an argument, at length, that the price of gold should be revalued to $70 an ounce to counter the inflation which had already taken place, in order to stop further deterioration in the purchasing power of the dollar. Minca immediately grasped the point and pointed to this argument in support of her own position that it is gold that should be acquired rather than corporate stock. I pointed out to Minca that freezing money in gold which yields no income is a sterile investment and, certainly at that point in time, did not seem to be a desirable thing to do. Although even then I did concede that at some time, probably not in the distant future, the argument advanced by Mr. Janeway would become valid, but that there was plenty of time to wait until the alternative of gold should be considered. Little did I realize that before the end of the decade of the 60's such time would approach.

Let us now move forward to the spring of 1970. The disastrous events which had taken place in 1969 involving a drop in securities values and the failure of major brokerage houses was fresh in everybody's mind. We had a small dinner party in our home at which was present a young man whom I shall call Bert. He had behind him years of experience with brokerage houses and in the five years between 1964 and 1969 he had an enviable record of success in the development of the business of a brokerage house in a foreign country where the prospect of attracting investors had not been regarded as very promising. Early in 1969 he had foreseen what was going to happen during the year and felt that he did not want to be in the position of inviting people to invest in the American stock market in view of what his prescience told him. He resigned his position and came back to the United States. Events had borne out the correctness of his judgment.

Also present was a somewhat older man whom I

shall call Frank. As an investment advisor and broker he managed several large portolios. His success had brought him the confidence of a number of very wealthy men. Frank is an intelligent and experienced investment advisor, firmly grounded in economics and stock analysis. He had twenty-five years of experience behind him and his thinking had always been in conventional stock analysis and economic interpretation.

Recalling the clarity with which Bert had foreseen the debacle which had overtaken Wall Street —which was still in progress—I asked him his opinion as to what would take place from then on. Bert unhesitatingly expressed the view that future developments in the economy and the financial markets portended disaster. At that time, in May, 1970, he expressed the view that within a year-and-a-half there would be a very grave financial crisis, international in scope, which would result in a substantial devaluation of the dollar. He expressed the view that, at that time, May, 1970, one should invest only in silver bullion and since gold bullion was not permissible to American investors, then to buy gold coins, some of which were legal to own, Canadian and American gold stocks and South African gold stocks.

As he talked, giving his cogent reasons for coming to this conclusion, I vividly recalled the radio interview with Eliot Janeway described above. All of my thinking fell into place and I recognized on the instant the correctness of Bert's analysis and realized that now had come the time which I told Minca would eventually arrive.

Frank expressed astonishment at Bert's view

and my concurrence. He asked "What do you think the price of gold will be?" Unhesitatingly, my thoughts fell into place and I responded by saying that the price of gold at that time should be $140 per ounce. In shocked disbelief Frank asked how I had arrived at what seemed to him to be an absurd figure. I immediately responded by pointing out that almost all prices of goods and commodities at that time, the spring of 1970, were four times what they had been, when gold was fixed at $35 per ounce in February, 1934, and there was no reason for the most universally desired commodity to be priced so far behind.

It speaks well for Frank that despite his shocked disbelief he sent me the next day, a study of South African gold stocks which had been made a year or two earlier by an analyst in his brokerage firm.

The discussion that took place that night prompted me to take immediate action. I familiarized myself with the available gold stock investments contained in the study that Frank sent me and I consulted with a number of friends of mine whose intelligence and economic thinking I respected. Not one of those to whom I spoke concurred with Bert's view in any way whatsoever. Indeed, one of my friends who had taught economics at a leading university and who had a successful record of investing his own funds so that from poverty he had become a millionaire, told me he agreed with studies he had read which indicated that if gold were demonetized it would be worth no more than $8 an ounce. Others with whom I spoke had not given the subject any thought and were completely skeptical at all the arguments which I advanced. Nevertheless, I persisted and discovered that there were a number of financial writers who did have the view that investment in gold was desirable. They were known in the Wall Street community as "gold bugs." A review of what they had written indicated that, like Janeway, they had all become gold bugs at too early a date. Indeed, if they had been listened to over the preceding years, one would perhaps have had substantial losses in missed opportunities in other forms of investments. But the more I read them, the more I realized that while they had come to their gold-bug view too early, the time had now arrived when it seemed likely that they would be right. Being of a cautious nature, with a full realization of how difficult it is to foretell the future, I decided to invest in gold stocks, but not to go the whole hog as Bert had recommended. Accordingly I sold the bonds I owned which at that time were yielding incredibly high returns measured by past records and bought a diversified portfolio of dividend-yielding South African gold mining shares.

Neither Bert nor I expected that our judgment would be vindicated so soon. The monetary crisis which Bert had foreseen and expected to take place in a year-and-a-half actually developed in the summer of 1971.

The moment of truth finally arrived on August 15, 1971 when President Nixon announced the suspension of dollar convertibility. At the same time the dollar was devalued in terms of gold from $35 to $38 an ounce, and this was formally recognized by the Smithsonian agreement of December

18, 1971.

All too soon, subsequent developments indicated that this had been an insufficient devaluation and another financial crisis developed in 1973 which resulted in another ten percent devaluation on February 12, 1973 which raised the official price of gold to $42.22 per ounce.

At this point, it should be noted that economic events often take a long time to work themselves out. During the ensuing years I saw the price of the gold stocks I had bought drop precipitously in value then come back, drop again, and then go forward. In the meantime, though, I remained convinced that the fundamental reasons still existed, even more strongly, for acquiring the gold stocks, and in the meantime I was being paid substantial dividends.

But my personal story does not end here. In February, 1972 I was called upon to handle an estate of which the two chief beneficiaries were brothers, whom I will call respectively William and Charles. They were also the executors of the estate and their share of the inheritance amounted to about $100,000 each. The assets of the estate consisted entirely of high grade corporate stocks. Indeed the value of the estate was due almost entirely to successful investing in securities. At this point, I should note that the two brothers, William and Charles were very disparate in their life styles. Charles was a professor of history, while William was a successful business man.

Their father had died in February, 1972. Charles and William were appointed executors in April. Almost immediately a serious difference developed between them. The stock market had begun to decline. Charles urgently demanded that all the securities in the estate be sold while William insisted on holding on to them. I asked Charles why he was so insistent on selling so quickly. He explained that he desired to invest the inheritance in gold and gold-related securities. Giving his reasoning, he explained that his income was more than sufficient for current needs. In addition he was protected for the normal future by the expectation of a generous pension plus social security. However, Charles was disturbed by the progress of events in the world and he sensed at least the possibility of disastrous occurrences in the future. Since the inheritance was of no immediate use for his current needs, he felt that he should invest in the one thing which in his judgment would have value if all else collapsed—namely, gold and gold related investments. William was in total disagreement with this view.

The securities in the estate were sold. William reinvested his inheritance in good quality stocks and bonds. Charles bought gold coins and South African gold stock.

Need I say what has happened in the intervening two years? Charles' investment has more than tripled in value, while William's is worth little more than half.

Chapter III

What Is Money?

"What is money?" strikes one as a foolish question at first blush. The answer seems obvious—money is the paper bills and the metal coins in our pockets and the figures printed into our bank books when we give the teller at the bank some of those bills and coins.

Alas, this obvious response is but a small part of the answer to the question "What is money?" Indeed, the answer is so complex that it rivals the difficulties of theoretical physics or higher mathematics. In fact, through the ages—and to this day —economists are in grave disagreement as to how to define money and even more so as to how to understand the way it works. Yet, in order to make our own personal decisions whether or not to invest in gold we *must* give some thought to the nature of money.

The first Biblical reference to money is at Genesis XXIII:16:

"Abraham weighed to Ephron the silver which he had named in the audience of the children of Heth, four hundred shekels of silver, current money with the merchant to buy the field of Machpelah with its cave to bury Sarah and his family."

Yet a little further on in Chapter XXX of Genesis it is related that Abraham's grandson, Jacob, worked for his father-in-law, Laban, for seven years and that he was paid by the transfer to him of all of the spotted and speckled sheep of Laban's flock.

Indeed, the earliest form of money appears to have been domestic animals and the "talent" mentioned in Homer was the amount of gold figured to be equal to the value of one ox.

In much later times we have the story of the purchase of Manhattan Island from the Indians by the Dutch for a box of beads.

In different times and places a great variety of things have been used for money—stones, shells, ivory, wampum, beads, tobacco, furs, dried fish, cigarettes—and above all, silver and gold. Precious metals, early in the development of civilization, were used for money because of convenience, durability, divisibility and the high intrinsic value which people placed on them.

The importance of money in the development of civilization is that it provided a flexible means of engaging in commercial activities over the more primitive and cumbersome systems of barter.

But all of the foregoing tells us only what has been used for money. It does not answer the fundamental question "What is money?"

Let us look at some of the modern views of "What is money?":

(1) It is the medium in which prices are expressed.

(2) When it is established by law as "legal tender," it is the means used for the discharge of debts.

(3) It is what is used to buy goods and pay for services.

(4) It is what is used as bank reserves.

(5) Some modern economists define "money supply" as "common money" which is made up of currency (money issued by the government or its authorized bank, consisting of bank notes and coins), *plus* demand deposits in banks (that is, deposits on which checks can be drawn).

(6) In a broader sense the word is defined to include things that do not necessarily enter into circulation, such as "standard money," namely, what is held by countries as a basic monetary reserve. In the United States this would include gold certificates in the reserves of the Federal Reserve banks and deposits at the reserve banks held for member banks.

(7) Recently the monetary authorities of the Western countries created a wholly new kind of money called Special Drawing Rights (SDRs) which exist as bookkeeping entries under the auspices of the International Monetary Fund. Although apparently created out of thin air, they are now part of the world's

basic monetary reserves.

(8) The term "money" may even be used for abstract, non-existent units such as the "guinea" in which some prices are expressed in England—even though no actual "guinea" has been circulating for many years.

(9) "Near money" is an expression used for such things as time deposits and short term government obligations because they have some of the characteristics of money and affect the way the monetary system works.

(10) Money is the unit of account in which records are kept, costs computed and values compared.

(11) Money is that which serves as the reserves of easily usable purchasing power and is thus the only completely liquid asset.

(12) Money, in forms other than gold and silver, is not generally regarded as wealth itself but as a means of storing and measuring wealth (an increase in the quantity of money in a country does not necessarily increase its wealth but may be only a symptom of inflation).

(13) Money, as such, is neither a good nor a consumption good.

(14) Money is used as a *numeraire*, something which serves for counting or expressing value.

(15) The transition from the use of the word money to mean commodity value to also embrace debt, was very important in the development of money.

(16) Today, debt money has no convertibility into

a commodity. The most common form of debt money is checkbook money.

(17) The nature, form and use of money is constantly changing, as witness the rise in the use of credit cards and computer account entries for many of the functions of money.

As a practical matter there are two aspects of money which are of basic interest for the average man who is not a banker, economist, Treasury Department official or statesman.

First, he thinks of money as a medium of exchange. What useful goods such as real estate, automobiles, food, clothing or shares in a business (stocks) can he buy with the otherwise useless paper or bits of metal in his pocket, or recorded in his bank account? Or, if he sells something of real value, how much of this paper or metal can he get?

Secondly, he thinks of money as a store of value. Since the paper bills or the bits of metal or the records at his bank permit him to buy goods or services he needs or wants, he thinks of accumulating this purchasing power and generally, without thinking more about it, regards the accumulation of such paper bills, bits of metal or bank recordings as the storing up of purchasing power and a measure of his wealth. These two fundamental aspects of money are interrelated. Over the years the most widely used means of giving stability to both the purchasing power aspect and the store of value aspect of money was the use of the gold standard or a combination of gold and silver (bimetallism) whereby the paper bills, bits of metal or bank notations could be converted into a commodity of universally recognized value—gold or silver. Under a gold standard a domestic currency will be equal in value to a specified amount of gold all over the world. The gold standard gives stability and dependability to money; and its convertibility into some of the essentially limited amount of gold and silver in the world prevents the government from unlimited issuance of money.

For a number of years before 1933, the United States was on a true gold standard because the paper bills and bits of metal were freely exchangeable into gold. Beginning in 1934, the United States went on a "gold exchange standard" whereby the individual citizen could no longer have the privilege of free convertibility; but gold was exchanged between governments when the external trade resulted in imbalances of currency accumulations. The gold exchange standard provided the necessary two-way market for gold so that an equilibrium of currencies and trade could be maintained.

The virtues of the gold standard, and even of the gold exchange standard, are that it limits the power of governments to inflate the currency by printing an excessive amount and it creates certainty in international trade because it keeps stability in the exchange rate (the ratio of the value of one country's currency to that of others). This is the so-called "disciplinary power" of gold.

The dollar price of gold was finally unpegged in 1971-1972 with a consequent freeing of international exchange rates from the discipline of gold, and resulted in the "floating" or unstable situation we have today, with all its inflationary consequences.

When currency is not convertible in fixed terms into gold (or any other specific commodity or combination of commodities), it is then said to be on a "paper standard." The value of such paper standard money then must rely on governmental self-control and strict regulation. The maintenance of some semblance of value in this kind of money often depends on multiple exchange rates between countries and such things as the use of exchange stabilization funds.

The foregoing is an extremely brief consideration of matters which are the subjects of learned books by writers who disagree more often than not in both theory and practical considerations.

However, it is important for anyone considering whether to invest in gold to keep in mind the complex nature of money and to realize that even the most profound thinkers on the subject differ widely in their conclusions concerning all aspects of the subject.

This leads to one important clear conclusion: That the value of money—especially paper standard money—is based on a mystique.

Charles R. Whittlesey, Professor of Finance, University of Pennsylvania, a leading thinker in the field of money theory, points out that even after the collapse of the international gold standard in the 1930's, the world continued to trade with money that had no commodity value, with no prospect of convertibility into a money commodity, and yet managed to maintain a trade value. He points out that at bottom "money is accepted because it is accepted." The exchange value of money appears not to derive from some prior dependent value but as a quality emanating from money as money. Such value is really a reflection of the value of goods and services for which it is exchangeable and really, in the end, depends upon the behavioral quality of *acceptability* which is a question of social behavior or custom. In other words money, like poker chips, has value only because it will be accepted by others.

There is infinitely more to monetary theory than has been discussed—the relation between money and prices, quantity theory, the meaning and effect of velocity or turnover of money, income-expenditure analysis, monetary policy, international aspects of money—and much more.

But for this discussion it is most important to keep in mind that under the prevailing paper standard money system—wholly dependent on the restraints and safeguards of government—the value of the paper bills and bits of metal in our pockets and the notations in our bank accounts is based on one thing—acceptability or *mystique*.

A dramatic example of this mystique element in money is provided by the story of how the German mark was stabilized after the nightmare inflation during the early 1920's which saw the Reichsbank, by October, 1923, printing 120,000 trillion marks *a day*; while demand far outstripped that figure—such demand was for one million trillion marks a day. But in November 1923 currency reform began. The Rentenbank was established to issue a brand new currency called the Rentenmark. The Rentenmark was freely convertible into bonds backed by land and factories. About two-and-one-half billion Rentenmarks valued at one trillion old paper marks were issued. Abruptly inflation ceased and the Rentenmarks held their value. How could this have happened when there was a new money supply whose backing by real estate was essentially a friction since there was no way to foreclose or distribute it? The answer is that the government induced the people to have *confidence* (mystique?) by announcing that the new currency would be held stable in value; the real estate backing gave the *illusion* of value and, in fact, the government strictly limited the amount of Rentenmarks to be issued while it halted the issue and discounting of paper marks. In their hunger for usable money, the people extended the benefit of the doubt to the new Rentenmark. This gave the government time in the ensuing months to take steps to consolidate the new *confidence* by the adoption of reasonable credit policies and, finally, to restore a 30% gold backing —though not convertibility.

It is necessary to realize the importance of the mystique element in money because those economists who seek to throw gold out of the monetary system use as one of their chief arguments that gold's value is only due to its mystique.

Chapter IV

What Is Inflation?

In order to make a decision whether you want to invest in gold you must give some consideration to the difficult question of inflation, its nature, causes, history and remedies, if any.

We all know the effects of inflation—we learn the hard way, and we continue to learn whenever we go shopping. But a little review won't hurt, if only to put things in perspective.

On February 1st, 1934, President Roosevelt raised the price of gold from $20 per ounce and pegged it at $35. On that day, as reported in the *New York Times*, the commodities futures market showed silver at forty-four cents an ounce, coffee at seven cents a pound, copper, seven cents, cotton seed oil, five cents. The advertisements in that day's paper showed Finchley selling men's suits (on sale since it was mid-winter) at thirty-one dollars, Weber & Heilbroner reduced men's hats from five dollars to two dollars and ninety-five cents, Ben Marden at his then famous night club was presenting Ethel Waters with show, dinner, and continuous dancing for two dollars and twenty-five cents, and a seat at a matinee of the Ziegfeld Follies ranged from one dollar to two fifty. The Holland America Line offered a six day cruise for seventy-five dollars.

Although the study of inflation in depth is, like money, a very abstruse subject it is obvious that, in essence, inflation is one thing—rising prices or, concomitantly, an increase in the cost of living.

Similarly, in simple terms, the cause of inflation is one thing—an increase in the supply of money which exceeds the quantity of goods and services available to spend it on, so prices go up and the value of money goes down.

What causes the increase in the money supply? Ah, there's the rub: to answer this question we must leave the realm of simplicity. Let's take a brief look at the past. In the ancient Greek world the basic money supply was based on silver. The Greek talent was divided into sixty minae, and the mina into one hundred drachmae (scholars tell us the drachma was the equivalent of about one dollar). Will Durant, quoting G. Glotz "Ancient Greece at Work," tells us that at the close of the fourth century B.C. prices were five times as high as at the opening of the sixth; they doubled again from 480 to 404 and there was another doubling from 404 to 330.

Solon (an Athenian ruler who lived from 640 to 558 B.C.), according to Plutarch "made the mina, which before passed for seventy-three drachmas go for a hundred, so that, though the number of pieces in the payment was equal, the value was less; which proved a considerable benefit to those that were to discharge great debts and no loss to the creditors." (Historians interpret this to mean that Solon had depreciated the currency by twenty-seven per cent, but this did not hurt the landlords too much because their own debts were payable in the debased currency.) Here we have an example of inflation caused by a fiat increase in the money supply, equivalent to printing more money today.

But the money supply can increase in other ways—even a sudden increase in the gold supply can cause inflation. This appears to have occurred in Alexander's Greece when his conquest of the East, especially the treasury of Darius at Persepolis flooded Greece with huge quantities of gold and silver. Again this happened in the sixteenth century in Spain when the American conquest brought in huge quantities of gold and silver. Instead of investing this new purchasing power in development so as to increase production, the beneficiaries of the new wealth, chiefly the nobility, added to their land holdings, paid for wars and bought huge annuities. Prices rose and the burden fell on the middle class and peasants. Spain never fully recovered from the sterile inflation brought about by this new-found gold.

Will Durant tells us that in Europe at the time of the Reformation:

"The new supplies of gold and silver cried out for profitable investment; American gold became European capital . . .

"The new wealth was largely confined to the merchants, financiers, manufacturers and their allies in government . . . The proletariat shared with the nobility the penalties of inflation. From 1500 to 1600 the price of wheat, with which the poor baked their bread, rose 150% in England, 200% in France, 300% in Germany. Eggs had been 4d for ten dozen in England in 1300; in 1400 the same quantity cost 5d; in 1500, 7d; and in 1570, 42d. Wages rose, but more slowly since they were regulated by government. In England the law (1563) fixed the annual wage of a hired farmer at twelve dollars, of a farm hand at nine dollars fifty, of a 'manservant' at seven dollars twenty-five. Allowing for the purchasing power of these sums to have been twenty-five times greater in 1563 than in 1954, they came to a hundred and eighty dollars or so per year. We should note, however, that in all these cases bed and board were added to the wage. By and large the economic changes in the sixteenth century left the working classes relatively poorer, and politically weaker, than before."

Somewhat analagous to the inflation caused by the sudden increase of the money supply in Spain and Europe; at the present time, is the vast influx of United States dollars to Europe in the 1950's and 1960's which has produced so much inflation there.

However, the most common cause of inflation —excessive increase in the money supply—is usually debasement of the currency.

In describing the economic decline of Rome, Will Durant writes:

"Financial difficulties entered. The precious metals were running low. The gold mines of Thrace and the silver mines of Spain had reduced their yield, and Dacia, with its gold, would soon be surrendered by Aurelian. Much gold and silver had been consumed in art and ornament. Faced with this dearth when war was almost continuous, the emperors from Septimus Severus onward repeatedly debased the currency to pay for state expenses and military supplies. Under Nero the alloy in the denarius was ten percent. Under Commodus thirty, under Septimus fifty. Caracalla replaced it with the antoninianus containing fifty percent silver; by 260 its silver content had sunk to five percent. The government mints issued unprecedented quantities of cheap coin; in many instances the state compelled the acceptance of these at their face value instead of their actual worth, while it insisted that taxes should be paid in goods or gold. Price rose rapidly; in Palestine they increased 1,000 percent between the first and third centuries; in Egypt inflation ran out of control, so that a measure of wheat that cost eight drachmas in the first century cost one-hundred twenty thousand at the end of the third. Other provinces suffered much less; but in most of them inflation ruined the large part of the middle class, nullified trust funds and charitable foundations, rendered business discouragingly precarious, and destroyed a considerable portion of the trading and investment capital upon which the economic life of the Empire depended."

Let us come to more modern times. In 1793, the new regime installed after the French Revolution, finding itself threatened by invasion by the monarchical regimes abroad and from rebellion within, began to issue nonconvertible paper money called the *assignat*. For a while their value was maintained by wage and price controls. But these were ineffective, and the standard of living dropped as prices went up. In December, 1794, controls were abolished. Floods of *assignats* were placed in circulation with accompanying steep price rises. The *assignats* lost 68% of their face value in May 1795, and 97% in July. Investors were ruined and workers reduced to near starvation. The decline of the *assignat* continued so that the cost of living in Paris, by November 1795, was 50 times what it had been in 1790.

Earlier, a similar inflation was experienced by the newly born United States. To finance the Revolutionary War, the Continental Congress issued fiat (inconvertible) money called Continentals. They declined in value rapidly, and by 1780 the Continental Congress itself agreed that the Provisional Government would accept them at a fortieth of their face value. Soon after that nobody accepted them. Thus the expression: "Not worth a continental." By the end of the Revolutionary War, economic affairs were in a turmoil, largely due to the failure of the monetary system. Social upheaval, exemplified by Shay's Rebellion, threatened. James Madison said that the pressures resulting from economic disorder "contributed more to the uneasiness which produced the Constitution, and prepared the public's mind for a general reform" than any other deficiencies of the Articles of Confederation.

The United States again had the experience of runaway inflation during and after the Civil War. In 1862 the government issued inconvertible legal tender notes, popularly called "Greenbacks," which were given parity with metal-backed notes. By the end of the fighting, there were 450 million dollars of such greenbacks in circulation. They depreciated rapidly, and by the middle of 1864 were passing in circulation for 39% of the gold dollar. They did not return to acceptance at par value until 1879, when they were put on a gold basis by the Treasury's acquisition of a hundred million dollars of gold bullion.

The years following both World War I and World War II witnessed horrendous inflations resulting from the printing of excessive amounts of currency. The Austrian, Hungarian and Polish currencies were eventually stabilized at rates of from 14,000 to 1, up to 1,180,000 to 1, while the currencies of many other European countries lost from 75% to 99% of their pre-War purchasing power. The most publicized hyperinflation in modern times was that of Germany from mid-1922 to November 1923. The following table tells the story:

DATE	WHOLESALE PRICE INDEX
July 1914	1.0
January 1919	2.6
July 1919	3.4
January 1920	12.6
January 1921	14.4
July 1921	14.3
January 1922	36.7

July 1922	100.6
January 1923	2,785.0
July 1923	194,000.0
November 1923	726,000,000,000.0

By late 1923, 300 paper mills were producing at full speed, and 150 printing companies operating 2,000 presses were working day and night printing currency. By mid-1923 workers were being paid as often as three times a day. Shops emptied of goods. Farmers refused to sell for worthless paper. Businesses closed down and unemployment soared.

All the gory details are available in studies which scholars have made of this phenomenon. Suffice it to say that people depending on fixed incomes found themselves destitute after selling their furniture, clothing, jewelry, and art objects. Endowed institutions such as hospitals, charitable and religious institutions, closed as their funds became worthless.

After the "miracle of the Rentenmark" described in the previous chapter, the middle classes found themselves ruined while the workers were left disillusioned with the liberal democracy that had caused them so much suffering. The workers turned to communism and the bulk of the population provided fertile soil for Nazism. The showdown between Hitler and communism came in 1933—and the rest is history. A most important fact to be observed is that despite the astronomical increase in the face value of the currency in circulation, its true value when calculated in gold, fell, from 7,428 million marks in January 1920, to only

168 million marks by July 1923.

The economist, John Maynard Keynes, has shown that when people lose confidence in the currency, they spend it immediately, and this speeds up the circulation so that prices rise faster than new money can be printed. The economist, Alfred Marshall, studying this process, concluded that "the total value of inconvertible paper currency cannot be increased by increasing its quantity; any increase in quantity which seems likely to be repeated, will lower the value of each unit more than in proportion to the increase."

In the days immediately following World War II, a similar inflation gripped many countries of the world.

Australia, Venezuela, New Zealand, South Africa and Norway saw prices increase from 70 to 80%. In Canada, Switzerland, Costa Rica, U.S.A., and the United Kingdom, prices rose between 116 and 120%.

In Czechoslovakia, Spain, Egypt, India, Chile, Palestine, Belgium, Turkey, Iran and Brazil, the increase was from 220 to 400%.

Bulgaria, Finland, France, Japan and Poland had increases of several thousand percent. Countries with a German-type hyperinflation far exceeding the others mentioned were Greece, Hungary, Romania and China.

One economist expresses the view that inflations of up to 500% are possibly containable—but above that, not even a strong government can avoid being swamped.

We are now in the midst of a serious inflation which is gripping all the capitalist countries. Let us review what has happened.

The leading Western states, in conference assembled at Bretton Woods in 1944, established an international monetary system to govern international monetary payments in a manner providing reasonable stability to the value of their currencies. It was agreed that exchange rates would be fixed within limits of 1% fluctuation; that values for each currency would be declared in terms of United States dollars or gold at the United States rate of $35 per ounce; and to alter values more than 1% only to correct fundamental disequilibrium; and then in accordance with the rigidly specified procedures. The fundamental basis of the entire system was the reassurance of the United States to buy and sell gold (to central banks) at $35 per ounce.

Although the United States earned a surplus in foreign trade until 1971; from 1950 on, except for 1957, the United States suffered a deficit in its international balance of payments each year, usually ranging from one to four billion dollars annually. This resulted from a variety of complex reasons, but among them was spending overseas for military establishments and bases, the Korean and Vietnamese wars, investment abroad, especially by the large international corporations, legal and illegal transfers of legitimate individuals and the Mafia to banks abroad, and tourism. For example, by the end of 1970, direct U.S. investment abroad amounted to over 78 billion dollars.

By 1957 the dollar had begun to weaken as the United States monetary stock declined while that of Europe, whose economy was burgeoning, grew rapidly. This caused other countries to begin to show a preference for gold rather than the once-prized dollar. By 1966, demands under the Bretton Woods procedures had reduced the United States gold reserves from 23 billion dollars to 13 billion (the French were particularly insistent on settlements in gold).

The first sign of serious trouble in the Bretton Woods system developed when Britain, for a variety of reasons, experienced difficulties with its internal economy which weakened its foreign trade position. In an attempt to maintain stability the pound was devalued in 1967 from $2.80 to $2.40.

This crack in the system led to a test of the firmness of the value of the dollar, so that by March 1968 huge demands for gold appeared on the gold market in London. It developed that no European countries were willing to sell gold, and the U.S. Treasury suddenly became reluctant to deplete its reserves any further.

The London gold market closed on October 15th, and on October 18th the so-called two-tier system was introduced. From then on, gold would be used at $35 for settlements between central banks, but would be allowed to trade freely in the gold market.

Eight months later, in March 1968, so many dollars were thrown on the market in West Germany that the authorities decided to stop supporting it and to let it go through the Bretton Woods floor. On November 10th, major currency markets closed for three days. The finance ministers of the Group of Ten met at Bonn, and arranged to lend massive amounts of the currencies in greatest demand to the United States to support the dollar. Troubles in France led to a run on its gold reserves, and in the summer of 1969 the franc was devalued by 11.1%.

It became more and more difficult for the dollar to hold its fixed value of $35 per ounce of gold, especially after it became necessary for West Germany to first float and then upvalue the mark by 9.3%. The monetary storm subsided for a year-and-a-half.

In the United States, inflation began to rear its ugly head. To stem it, the prime rate was raised to 8½%, a credit crunch developed, and the stock market fell. The credit crunch was abandoned. Again the dollar weakened, leading to a crisis in May 1971 as dollars were again dumped for the mark. Again the European money markets closed, this time for five days.

The Swiss upvalued the franc by 7.1%, and Austria the shilling by 5%. West Germany and the Netherlands allowed their currencies to float.

In the meantime on the free market, gold rose to as high as $42 an ounce by early 1969, then fell to $35 in early 1970, after which it began to rise again, reaching $42 in July 1971. All the while, central banks were cautiously cashing in dollars for gold at the official price of $35 an ounce at the paying-teller window of the United States Treasury.

During this period, the so-called Special Drawing Rights or SDRs, were devised, with each unit valued at $1 or 1/35th of an ounce of gold. Being valued in gold, these SDRs were acceptable to the central banks, but for this reason they insisted on hoarding them, just like their gold, thus defeating the purpose for which they were issued: namely, to provide liquidity (or more currency) to the international monetary system.

By August 1971 the United States economy was again in trouble—price rises followed by pay raises were increasing the inflation, and the balance of payments deficit was on its way to total 9.28 billion dollars for 1971. The Swiss limited the number of dollars it would permit into the country, the West German mark floated up to 8% premium, and gold sold for $44 per ounce on the London market. Meanwhile, other countries were becoming more and more reluctant to support the dollar. On August 15, 1971, President Nixon announced a series of measures seeking to strengthen the dollar, chief of which was the closure of the gold window at the Treasury—in other words, the dollar was now naked—inconvertible into gold or any other thing of intrinsic value. The Bretton Woods system had collapsed.

An attempt was made to patch the old system when at a conference at the Smithsonian Institution in Washington it was agreed that (nominally, now, since it remained inconvertible) the dollar would be devalued 8% in terms of gold.

Meanwhile in June of 1972, the free market price of gold reached $60 an ounce. At the same time in 1972, the United States money supply increased 11%, standing at 246.8 billion dollars at the end of the year, with a concomitant increase in the price level, while the balance of payments deficit continued at exorbitant amounts in 1972 and 1973. The Smithsonian agreement was not working, and new assaults on the dollar led to new crises, so that by February 12, 1973, the nominal value of the dollar was again devalued by 11% to $42.22 per ounce of gold. All to no avail—the price of gold rose to $94 per ounce on February 22, 1973.

Still the dollar refused to inspire confidence, and Federal Reserve Board chairman Arthur F. Burns, stated to Congress: "We live in a world now where confidence in paper currencies has declined . . . there has been a certain decline in discipline, and if we don't watch our step, we will have currency wars, political uncertainties, and businessmen will have great uncertainty about their future."

Negotiations continued among the governments and on March 12, 1973 at a meeting of the European Economic Community Finance Ministers, it was decided that the West German mark be upvalued again by 3% and then, with France, Belgium, the Netherlands, Luxemburg and Denmark, those currencies all be allowed collectively to float against the dollar; while the currencies of Italy, Britain and Ireland would be allowed to float individually.

This was the end of the Bretton Woods Agreements, and the end of an era. From March, 1973 onwards the dollar was freed from all ties to gold and remained a naked token whose only real value lay in its mystique or "acceptability.' Since then, although the international monetary crises have subsided, many unsettling events have occurred.

From a price of $125 per ounce in June, 1973, gold rose to a high of $178 per ounce in early

1974. (It then retreated to as low as $130 an ounce —but probably on a temporary basis for technical reasons.)

The oil-exporting countries have quadrupled their prices.

There has been a sharp decline in the world's food stocks.

The Watergate affair has unsettled political and societal life in America with a depressing psychological impact on confidence.

Wage and price controls have proven ineffective in combating inflation leaving economists and monetary authorities at a loss as to how to restrain the ever-increasing inflation.

Again in June 1974, in a less crisis-ridden atmosphere after an earlier inconclusive meeting in Nairobi, the International Monetary Fund's Committee of Twenty met at Williamsburg, Virginia. While the conference failed to reach an agreement on the basic monetary problems facing the capitalist world, they at least agreed on some interim steps, mostly expressions of good intention. However, two significant moves were made. It was agreed to value SDRs, severing their link to gold and substituting a "bundle of currencies" for their valuation. To anyone fearful of inconvertible currency, this could only be regarded as portending further inflation on a global scale. It is difficult to understand how a bundle of deteriorating currencies could be used to bolster the world's financial system.

The other significant step is more encouraging. Despite the insistence of the United States on severing the monetary system from gold, it was agreed, with the concurrence of the United States, that countries could expand their borrowing power, using gold as collateral, *at a market-related price*.

Meanwhile world-wide inflation continues unabated. In ten countries, including Germany, France, Britain, Italy, Holland, Belgium, Denmark, Ireland, United States, and Japan it has ranged from 7%, in Germany and Belgium to 13%, in Japan—averaging out at 9.25% (in the United States—8%). These figures are for the year 1973; however these inflation rates are now obsolete since much higher rates have taken hold in almost every one of these countries, and as we saw earlier the Labor Department reported that wholesale prices rose 17.8% for the 12 months ending August, 1974.

Based on the United States Labor Department Consumer Price Index, taking 1967 to equal 100, the rise has been from about 128 in January, 1973 to over 145 at the end of May, 1974, in an unbroken ascent. From July, 1973 through July, 1974, the Consumer Price Index rose 11%, and has continued to rise since then. It was disclosed on September 23, 1974, that in August consumer prices rose 1.3% or at an annual pace of 15.6%. In the meantime according to the Bureau of Labor Statistics, the real spendable weekly earnings of the average worker with three dependants, expressed in 1967 dollars declined from about $96 to about $91 by the end of August, 1974.

On September 13, 1974, Kenneth Rush, then White House economic coordinator indicated that the inflation rate might still be *above* 10 per cent at the end of the year. "The picture is not as optimistic as it was two or three months ago," he said.

And the worst part of the picture is that no one in authority seems to know what to do. *Time* Magazine devoted the cover story of its April 8, 1974 issue to an essay entitled "Seeking Antidotes to a Global Plague." It says "So far, the global inflation virus has defied all attempts at treatment. The United States, most European countries and Japan have all experimented—halfheartedly to be sure—with some form of wage-price controls, tax and monetary tinkering or high interest rates; nothing has worked for long." It goes on to say ". . . some strong inflationary forces are working to keep the inflationary fever burning. Round the world, a growing number of jittery investors have lost confidence in the value of paper money . . . Certainly the record of major governments in dealing with inflation gives the world's consumer little reason to trust anything they say about prices. For the most part, it is a story of weak, erratic and often misdirected policies."

Asking how this happened and what to do, it answers "The antidotes to inflation have proved to be particularly elusive because the causes are deep and pervasive—and often unrecognized." It cites the view of World Bank Economist, Irving Friedman, who believes that the chilling unemployment and other events of the depression of the 30's have caused governments in effect to enter into a new social contract with their citizens to avoid such suffering at all costs. The article goes on to say that "in practice, the commitment has meant that governments, using the tools of Keynesian economics, react to anything but the briefest and shallowest down turn by increasing spending and pumping up the money supply in order to get the economy moving again."

The essay goes on to say: "Faced with these pressures, some economists throw up their hands and contend that the best way to deal with inflation is to accept it as permanent and make adjustment to anesthetize the pain. That is a counsel of despair. Such an approach tends to make, say a 6% inflation rate acceptable—and with that established as a base, other pressures will push the real rate to 8%, 10% and on up.

"At the other extreme, some economists argue for 'putting the economy through a wringer'—depressing demand enough to bring down prices, at whatever cost in unemployment. That is no answer at all; in the U.S., a 12% to 13% jobless rate for up to a year might be required to bring inflation down to an annual pace of about 2%, and the human suffering caused would be greater than the pain of price increases."

Later on, the essay goes on to say:

"Yet the fight against inflation cannot be given up. Left unchecked, inflation pries wide whatever cracks already exist in a society. Prolonged inflation represents a failure, and that failure breeds edginess and mistrust. In time it becomes impossible for leaders to succeed because voters demand that government deal with inflation. Yet so various and insistent are the people's other special demands for higher government spending and inflation continues. As Economist Friedman writes: 'In virtually all cases of major political upheaval in the postwar period, inflation has been a common element.' "

In conclusion, the *Time* article makes several general suggestions but admits that none of the suggested steps can cure inflation.

The June 15th, 1974 issue of *Business Week* carried a six-page article entitled "An Expensive Gamble to Slow Inflation" in which it discusses the role of Federal Reserve Board Chairman Arthur Burns in pursuing monetary policy to ameliorate the rampant inflation. The following exerpts from the *Business Week* article give some idea of why inflation is unlikely to be stopped.

". . . What Burns believes is needed is a prolonged period in which money remains expensive and hard to find—a period that will last not weeks or months, but years. His goal is to return to relative price stability, and he believes that to achieve it there must be a long period of slow growth in the American economy—carefully controlled and measured by the Fed.

"It is a perilous policy, this business of imposing continued restraints on a financial system that is already dangerously short of liquidity. Indeed, it is questionable whether monetary policy is the appropriate weapon to deal with an inflation that is due in part to shortages and in part to price hikes in such cartel-controlled commodities as oil . . .

"There are problems in the domestic financial markets, beginning with the Franklin National Bank, 20th largest in the land until it ran into monumental trouble a month ago . . .

"Though it is hard to prove, other financial institutions are believed to be in some degree of trouble . . . then, of course, there are the utilities the biggest borrowers of all. They, too, are finding it deathly hard to keep raising all the money they need.

"The longer the Fed keeps applying the restraint, the greater the danger to all of these institutions. Burns and his Fed colleagues realize that their policy will produce casualties, that a number of marginal, weakly financed companies are going to fall by the wayside in the months to come . . .

"This strain is being felt beyond the domestic financial markets, as well. Nerves are strained in the vast Eurodollar market—the $150 billion market in dollars on deposit outside the United States . . .

"Inflation threatens to tear apart not only the economy, but American society, and only Burns and his Fed seem to be doing anything about it. Burns stands as a titanic figure at a time when official Washington is woefully short of such figures . . .

"Inflation, however, will be slow to fade, and the impact of Fed policy will be showing up more and more in the months ahead . . .

"Next year could be highly critical because the end of wage controls last April 30 could bring on a huge round of wage increases as workers try to catch up with the bounding cost of living. Nixon administration officials figure that if the average 8% wage increase (including fringes) of 1974 jumps to 12% next year, the level of price inflation would also turn up—perhaps from 7% expected by year end to 8% or 9% . . .

"It does not seem that anyone outside the Fed is going to change Burns's mind either, because there really is not anyone outside the Fed able or willing to grapple with the Chairman . . .

"Certainly, no one within the administration has offered an alternative to monetary policy in dealing with inflation, and it seems highly unlikely at this point that anyone will . . .

"The Administration's entire economic policy team has a sorry look these days . . .

"In the end, what Burns is talking about is keeping policy tighter for what could be a lot longer than the Fed has ever tried before—and that takes the central bank into unknown territory. As he pursues this policy, Burns will have to reflect on the warning that one economist made some years ago. 'A restrictive monetary policy,' the man said, 'if pursued very long, will damage the economy.' Burns should remember that line very well since he was that economist, and then only an observer of the Fed, not its chairman."

Chapter V

Inflation Hedges

From all the foregoing, we must work on the assumption that the present high rate of inflation will continue to run on without any effective restraints from government policy or conscious public behavior.

This poses a tremendous problem for you if you have anything to invest and do not want to see your wealth—large or small—evaporated by the fires of inflation.

The problem is complicated by the fact that deflation (or depression) may suddenly call a halt to the inflationary process. This could mean that cash, bonds, and evidences of debt would turn out to be valuable. Or the present rapid inflation could turn into a hyperinflation, causing cash and cash equivalents to be worthless.

But the problem is even more complicated than either of those alternatives suggest. Many economists, who believe there is little chance of controlling or rolling back the inflationary process, believe we may avoid hyperinflation and still not have the crashing effects of a depression. They believe it is not only possible but likely that we are entering upon a period of high inflation coupled with recession. That is deteriorating currencies, diminishing or profitless business activity, lower profits, higher unemployment, a lifeless or unattractive stock market, sporadic but continuing bankruptcies, little real estate activity. A new word—stagflation—has been invented for this bleak prospect in which we would have the worst of both possible worlds—chronic rotting of our currency together with a gradually declining standard of living. In fact, at this writing we can see the beginning of the stagflation process—increasing rate of inflation and decline in the growth of the gross national product, both occurring simultaneously.

In all three of these situations, inflation, depression, stagflation—those who will be hurt the most will be people living on fixed incomes and those with some income to invest. What are the alternatives they face? What can they do with their money?

Let us consider some possible courses of action.

Fixed Dollar Investments

These are cash, bank accounts, treasury bills, certificates of deposit, government or corporate bonds, mortgages and the like.

It is obvious that with inflation this kind of wealth declines in value even though the number of dollars remains the same. If we have an inflation rate of from 10 to 25% a year (which many economists think is likely) it requires little calculation to see how quickly wealth in the form of fixed dollar investments evaporates. If hyperinflation sets in, then you can kiss goodbye to such money altogether.

Of course, in a depression, this sort of investment can turn out to be the best—although some kinds of such investments like corporate bonds and mortgages, personal debt, et cetera, may very well be defaulted.

Stocks and Mutual Funds

Of course, in a depression, this sort of investment has the firmness of wet sand. We all know what happened in 1929 and thereafter. Other crashes brought similar disasters to this kind of investment.

Traditionally, stocks have been regarded as inflation hedges and when, in recent years, we have had declining stock markets during an inflationary period analysts took a second look and made studies which indicated that over the long run—say 20 years—they still seem to keep the investor ahead of the game. Other studies have shown that over a longer period, stocks on the average, (God help you if you were unfortunate enough to be invested in other than the average) have increased in fixed dollar value at the overall rate of 9% per year. Now, if the overall rate of inflation during the same period was substantially lower than 9% then it would turn out that stocks were a good investment—even if not a great one.

But once inflation goes over the rate of 5% then stocks offer little refuge. And if we enter a period of stagflation, then we can have a declining or low level stock market eroding our investments while inflation erodes the remaining values even more.

Real Estate

Many people who have made a special study of real estate have earned fortunes—indeed it has been said that more money has been made in real estate than in the stock market.

But for the average investor, real estate has many disadvantages. It is illiquid, that is, it is not readily salable. Income property is vulnerable to the imposition of rent controls. In difficult times, tenants can become bankrupt or otherwise unable to pay their rent, and vacant property quickly builds up losses because the landlords' fixed expenses, such as mortgage payments, taxes, insurance, maintenance, et cetera continue—and concomitantly, values drop so that less can be realized on a sale than was paid for it.

Vacant land, properly located, can be a good investment in times of prosperity and well-being. In periods of high and rising inflation, with costs escalating, money scarce and interest high, builders hesitate to build, buyers are uncertain and refrain from purchases. In a deflation, no one builds, and land is dropped for taxes. The market disappears completely. In stagflation much the same is to be expected.

Of course, in the long run, over a period of generations, vacant land can be immensely profitable but this is for the very wealthy to consider. Recently I heard that a super-rich partnership bought 200,000 acres (more than 310 square miles) of a southwestern state for $50 an acre for a total investment of $10,000,000. In those brackets, vacant land might be a good place to park money for distant future profits.

Art, Antiques, Stamp and Coin Collections

This kind of investment has proven to be an exceptionally good one in mildly inflationary, prosperous times. Some people accumulate money at a fast rate, believe it will continue forever, and then feel free to indulge in what psychologists recognize as a natural urge, stronger in some than in others, to accumulate and collect. (Look up the Freudian explanation.) As prices rise they rationalize that such self-indulgence is also good business. Acquisitions accelerate and prices go up very quickly. We then see the breathtakingly high prices brought for a few square inches of painted canvas or a single square inch of postage stamp. In periods of deflation these prices melt like snow in the summertime. With rapidly rising inflation, or stagflation, people feel worried and even if they have a lot of money, they understand what inflationary erosion can do to it. They lose interest in favored possessions and seek to protect what capital they have so prices of such objects drop. In stagflation this process is likely to be even more pronounced.

Diamonds and Other Precious Jewels

This investment has some merit as a protection for wealth. However, the same considerations apply here as to works of art, even if in lesser degree. Furthermore, even if bought knowledgeably, there is immediate loss. You must expect that when you buy, the dealer will take a minimum of 10 percent, and the same when you sell. Also, it is common knowledge that the diamond market is strictly controlled by the South African producers, so that world-wide prices are maintained artificially. This maintenance of the market may not always be effective.

Diamonds are especially valuable for the storage of much wealth in a little space if one wants to move about quickly. They serve refugees well. All Europeans know people whose lives and fortunes have been saved by precious jewels.

Consumption Goods

This category comprises automobiles, household furnishings and appliances, clothing including fur coats, valuable rugs, and the like. In the face of inflation such goods always look well-bought as prices go higher. In deflation one has the satisfaction of possessing and using them.

I knew a fellow who made a fortune in the twenties. When the crash of 1929 came he lost all, and finally took a job for 35 dollars a week (believe it or not, a living then). But he was left in possession of fine furniture, a number of good Persian rugs, a new expensive luxury car, a fine wardrobe for himself and his wife, including two mink coats. All of this did much for the family's morale during parlous times.

In the same way a businessman may benefit from having invested in good, efficient, usable machinery and equipment.

Your Own Business

A well-situated, good business, dealing in basic needs, can be the best hedge of all—you will keep up with inflation, and ahead of deflation, if you work hard at it and are lucky. The same is also true of an established professional practice. On a lower scale, civil servants, with tenure, are reasonably well protected from the worst ravages of inflation, deflation, or stagflation.

Gold and Silver

When all is said and done, gold and, to a lesser degree, silver, provide the best inflation-deflation hedge: The reasons for this will be demonstrated later and a guide as to how to take advantage of gold and silver as wealth protection in uncertain times will be set forth.

Chapter VI

The Enemies of Gold

Religions see the world as the battleground of a war between the Powers of Darkness and the Powers of Light. In a similar way, economists tend to see the world as a struggle between "hard money" and "easy money." Gold is the ultimate hard money because of its universal acceptability since the dawn of history. The champions of hard money are those who seek economic stability and have something to lose—pensioners, creditors, savers, and all those who have managed to acquire some wealth. The proponents of easy money are generally debtors and those with few possessions. They have nothing to lose, and when money is made easier; that is, more plentiful, some of it manages to dribble down to them in the form of higher wages and easier repayment of debts.

Easy money would not be so bad if it could be kept within bounds, but history has shown, without exception, that this can never be accomplished for any extended period of time. When "easy money" prevails in the battle, it always gets drunk with victory and goes on to the excesses of inflation—which if not checked in time results in severe injury to or the destruction of money, and ultimately to panics, crashes, and all their accompanying disasters. This is what World Bank Economist Irving Friedman meant when he wrote: "In virtually all cases of major political upheaval in the postwar period, inflation has been a common element."

One of the main themes in American history of the 1800's is the struggle between "hard money" and "easy money." The Populists demanded easy money, and after the discovery of large quantities of silver in the American southwest it took the form of a demand for the free coinage of silver in the ratio of 16 to 1. This demand was that the price of an ounce of silver should be fixed at 1/16th the price accorded to an ounce of gold, and that money backed by silver, at that price, should be issued into circulation. Because of the new supplies of silver, this would result in a large increase of the money in circulation, and produce "easy money." The result would have been similar to the printing of inconvertible Greenbacks during the Civil War. This movement found its most dramatic expression in the oratory of William Jennings Bryan, the thrice-defeated Democratic candidate for the Presidency. In a celebrated speech he said:

"You come to us and tell us that the great cities are in favor of the gold standard; we reply that the great cities rest upon our broad and fertile prairies. Burn down your cities and leave our farms, and your cities will spring up again as if by magic; but destroy our farms and the grass will grow in the streets of every city in the country . . . Having behind us the producing masses of the nation and the world, supported by the commercial interests, the laboring interests and the toilers everywhere, we will answer their demand for a gold standard by saying to them: You shall not press down upon the brow of labor this crown of thorns, you shall not crucify mankind upon a cross of gold."

After the Great Depression of the 1930's had engulfed the United States and Europe, another attack was launched against gold. This time it took a more respectable form in the really profound intellectual work of a towering British economist, John Maynard Keynes, who in his 1936 masterwork, "General Theory of Employment, Interest and Money" (said by some to be as difficult to understand in depth as the work of Einstein), referred to gold as a "barbarous relic." He argued for a monetary system free from the restraints of gold and advocated the use by governments of two tools that were readily within government grasp—monetary policy and fiscal policy. Monetary policy refers to the power of government to issue money, fiat (inconvertible) or otherwise, the regulation of foreign exchange rates, and the flexible manipulation of interest rates. Fiscal policy includes taxation and budget-making (putting into surplus or deficit), also called debt management. Keynesian economists view these two types of policy as supplementary, with monetary policy more effective for containing inflation, and fiscal policy as more effective in overcoming deflation.

On a rarified intellectual level, the Keynesian thesis was little different from the demagoguery of Bryan. Both advocated getting rid of the sobering restraint of gold to make money easier. Keynes, of course, hoped that the discipline of gold could be discarded and the ravages of inflation avoided by the "fine tuning" processes his carefully worked out theories would provide. Alas, like Karl Marx before him, he failed to reckon with the frailty of human nature and the pragmatic result of pressures on the politicians who were to administer the monetary and fiscal policies. The ideas of Keynes had and continue to have great influence because they are so plausible, and their intended aim—easy money controlled exactly to meet the needs of the economy—so desirable. The failure of Keynesian policy is evident in the present world-wide rapid inflation resulting from attempts to put his theories into practice.

It should be noted that there are some who attribute the current inflation as being aggravated by the activities of the great American international corporations, thus making these worthy firms strange bedfellows (or, better, companions in arms) with the champions of "easy money." The argument is that after World War II, the dollar (convertible, at least between central banks, at $35 an ounce of gold) was undisputed king of currencies commanding unrivaled confidence around the world. With their dollars, the international corporations were able to buy plants and labor abroad at a fraction of the cost here in the United States. This enabled those companies to expand cheaply, produce cheaply, and grow at a fantastic pace. They obtained these dollars by means of huge bank credits (out of thin air) implicitly encouraged by the United States monetary authorities (the Treasury and the Federal Reserve Board). Such was the esteem in which the dollar was held and avidly sought abroad, that no one paid attention to the consequences of this activity—the huge balance of payments deficits run by the United States and the vast accumulation of dollars abroad (Eurodollars) until, as a consequence, foreign central banks, slowly at first, but with increasing rapidity, depleted the United States Treasury gold reserve from its initial 27 billion dollars after World War II to hardly more than 10 billion dollars in 1968, and a halt was called. The world was startled with the realization that this process had undermined the world monetary system by creating excess money, which was causing an uncontrollable inflation everywhere, with the world drowning in inconvertible currencies—cut off from all but a theoretical tie to gold.

(For the sake of completeness, some reference should be made to Lenin's antagonism to gold embodied in his comment that, in a Marxist world, gold would be of use only for making bathroom fixtures. The reasoning behind this has nothing to do with the struggle between "hard money" and "easy money" forces. It stems from the Marxist view that production should be for use

77

and not for profit; and that therefore there is no need for a "store of value," since under such a system, storage of value—wealth—would be forbidden.)

In addition to the above-described pressures for "easy money" there are a number of other considerations that have produced enemies of gold as a component of the monetary system. These considerations have been persuasive to the United States' monetary money managers.

1. It is argued that to put the currency back on a gold standard, the price must be much higher than the official $42 per ounce, and that this would increase the money supply and so add fuel to the fires of inflation.

2. In the political sphere, it would be disadvantageous, because it would increase the purchasing power of Russia, South Africa, and France, the world's largest holders of gold, outside the United States, and for whom the United States has little sympathy.

3. The argument is made that the United States has in the past given assurances that the monetary price of gold would never be raised; and that relying on these policies, many countries have held dollars in their monetary reserves so that an increase in the dollar price of gold would ruin the dollar as an international currency.

4. Even more fundamentally, the argument is made that the use of gold to support the monetary system is irrational, unscientific, and regressive. Ultimately this reasoning is based on the theories of Keynes, which in the abstract do have much appeal at first blush.

5. But most of all, the opposition to the resurrection of gold is that it hampers the freedom of the money managers of the government. That is, they seek to avoid the "discipline of gold." It is this constraint that has been the strongest ally of the forces of "easy money" and which has led to the present dangerous inflationary situation.

What is this discipline of gold, and how does it operate? When money is linked to gold exchange rates between the currencies of the various currencies their relationship remains fixed and pressures are produced to bring price levels into line. When imbalances occur, gold is shipped from one country to another, and this movement of gold tends to bring about a contraction in the currencies of those countries where the prices are high, and then expansion of currencies in countries where prices are low. Thus the expansion and contraction of currencies would depend on market forces, and not be subject to the will (or whim?) of the monetary authorities (in the United States, the Treasury and Federal Reserve Board).

In its July, 1973 study, the respected financial advisory service, "The International Bank Credit Analyst," published a study of gold, in the course of which a succinct description of this process was set forth:

"The discipline exercised by gold in effect is to raise the free market demand for gold—monetary and fabricated—above the level of new world supplies so that central banks must either lose gold or allow the free market price to rise. Over the past several years central banks have done both, losing gold on balance while being unable to prevent the price from rising dramatically. Such developments undermine the liquidity of central banks which in turn causes a deterioration in the quality of their liabilities—paper money. The rising premium on free market gold over the official price is a constant reminder that central bank paper is depreciating in a very real way and is thus continuing to erode confidence. In this way gold can still act as a discipline, even though no paper money in the world can actually be presented to its central bank for conversion into gold which has historically been the real discipline of convertibility.

"The basic economic laws of gold have been tested over many centuries. Governments have always responded in the same way to the embarrassment of facing the fact that their paper money cannot stand comparison with gold by resorting to controls, psychological warfare, and eventually severe penalties.

"The U.S., fitting into the standard mold, has tried for years to attack the symptom of the problem—the rising price of gold—through a variety of techniques to reduce the demand for gold and force others to hold its own paper, or paper substitutes such as SDRs, instead of gold. These monetary manipulations have always failed because the economic laws of gold and its historic disciplinary characteristics cannot be made to go away. Ultimately, gold market forces must prevail and gold will continue to exert its traditional role as store of value for wealth par excellence.

"Through the chaotic financial conditions of recent years and months one fact stands out clearly—the basic gold laws are just as valid as at any point in history, if not more so. The recent report suggesting that central banks will resume gold sales should be interpreted in this light. Such sales, if they were to take place, might alter the short-run supply and demand balance, but would do nothing to alter the basic rationale which makes gold and gold shares essential assets to hold in any portfolio geared to the long-run preservation of wealth."

The propaganda against gold and the ingrained thinking which has developed in the wake of the publication of the ideas of John Maynard Keynes, has become almost a hatred of gold as exemplified by the editorial attitude of the *New York Times*. On June 28, 1974, a lead editorial stated:

"It is extremely risky for Congress to be forcing the President's hand on gold at this time. Last month the United States ran a trade deficit of $777 million, the second largest in its history—the largest having been run in October, 1971, shortly before the dollar was devalued for the first time since 1933. A substantial outpouring of American dollars to buy gold bullion abroad could seriously worsen the trade and payments deficit that appears to many observers to lie ahead.

"Secretary of the Treasury Simon, who favors lifting the gold ban, has been vague about how much Treasury gold he would pay out before slamming the gold window on American citizens. Under these circumstances, a rapid rise in the price of gold could have a shattering effect on confidence in the dollar and other currencies. A rush to hoard gold could also hurt the domestic capital market as American citizens pulled their money out of savings accounts and turned away from investments in bonds and equities.

"At best, the clause fixing a year-end deadline for the lifting of the gold ban should be stricken from the bill. If that cannot be done without killing the United States contribution to I.D.A., then Congress should at minimum make clear its willingness to permit the Administration to postpone the prescribed lifting of the gold restrictions if in its judgment such action would endanger the nation's prosperity and balance of payments."

Again, on July 5, 1974, *the New York Times* editorialized:

"The price that some Congressmen exacted for supporting this responsible action, however, may be more than the nation can bear—or at least more than it can responsibly be asked to risk. Appended to the I.D.A. appropriation —in order to gain House votes—is a totally irrelevant provision that would permit Americans to buy, sell and own gold for the first time in forty years. The run on gold that this might touch off could have devastating effects on trade and payments balances abroad and on capital markets at home at a time when there is already perilous uncertainty on both fronts.

"The gold clause, which appears in slightly differing forms in the House and Senate versions of the I.D.A. bill, ought to be stricken in conference. At the very least, the conferees should empower the Administration to postpone the lifting of gold restrictions if in its judgment such action would endanger the nation's prosperity and balance of payments. In its present form, the potential risks of this measure unfortunately threaten to overwhelm the unquestionable merit of its original and fundamental purpose to fulfill the American commitment to I.D.A."

Chapter VII

Why Gold Must Win

It is a self-evident fact that gold is the one imperishable substance which from the dawn of civilization, in all times and places, has been regarded by humankind as having the ultimate in economic value. (Spiritual values are something else—indeed religious leaders, in opposing a materialistic outlook, never cease denouncing worldly overattachment to gold and what it stands for.) Very early in the Bible, Genesis II:10-12, we find that gold is mentioned as good:

> "And the river went out of Eden to water the garden; and from then it was parted, and became four heads. The name of the first is Pishon; that is it which compasseth the whole land of Havilah, where there is gold; and the gold of that land is good . . ."

Psalm 19 proclaims:

"The ordinances of Jehovah are true and righteous altogether. More to be desired are they than gold, yea than much fine gold; . . ."

And again, Proverbs 16:16: "Better get wisdom than gold."

Also, Peter I 1:7: "That the proof of your faith, being more precious than gold that perisheth."

But of worldly goods it is safe to say that from Inca chief to Roman emperor, from French tradesman to Indian peasant, nothing has stood the test of time as a store of value like gold.

The virtues of gold were sung by Premier Charles DeGaulle in a press conference on February 4, 1965:

". . . International exchanges must be established as was the case before the great world-wide disasters, on an unquestionable monetary basis which does not bear the mark of any individual country.

"What basis? Actually, it is difficult to envision in this regard any other criterion, any other standard than gold. Yes, gold, which does not change in nature, which can be made either into bars, ingots or coins, which has no nationality, which is considered, in all places and at all times, the immutable and fiduciary value par excellence. Furthermore, despite all that it was possible to imagine, say, write or do in the midst of major events, it is a fact that even today no currency has any value except by direct or indirect relation to gold, real or supposed. Doubtless, no one would think of dictating to any country how to manage its domestic affairs. But the supreme law, the golden rule . . . that must be enforced and honored again in international economic relations, is the duty to balance, from one monetary area to another, by effective inflows and outflows of gold, the balance of payments resulting from their exchanges."

Why is it that gold has possessed this universal confidence?

Those seeking to denigrate the role of gold sneeringly refer to this persistent attachment as a "mystique." But as we have seen above, all money finds its acceptance as an object of value on the basis of a mystique—it is acceptable because it is acceptable, because it is acceptable.

Proponents of gold have no difficulty in finding a real basis for the age-old respect for gold:

° Gold is scarce.

° Gold is infinitely durable.

° Gold is beautiful—and the supreme material for the manufacture of jewelry, for which there is a constant demand.

° Gold is expensive to mine and refine (even using a man-hour basis for computation).

° Gold is increasingly demanded in industrial processes which, because of increasing complexity (especially electronic equipment) are becoming more demanding of its special qualities such as resistance to corrosion, superior electrical conductivity, malleability and tensile qualities, all of which render it easy to work.

° Gold is compact and thus easily storable and portable.

° Gold is anonymous (it doesn't carry the replica of the signature of a politician).

° Gold is easily recognized and easily assayed.

° Gold through the ages has provided a measure of value and a means of conserving and using wealth independent of the fiat of governmental authorities—for this reason gold provides a means for the individual to free himself from governmental oppression.

As the economist and gold expert William H. Tehan of Herzig and Co. said recently:

". . . If we could own gold, then we would be more independent of government, and with the mountain of debt that the United States government has, and the rate of taxation that we have, which I think is going to increase substantially, gold offers too much freedom, too much opportunity to hide capital."

Or, as in the same discussion, Franz Pick, the respected investment advisor, said:

"And I would like to say, to make a long story very short, what will remain of all the nonsense that we have committed, and with which we have infected the world, is nothing but gold, silver, platinum, and palladium.

Because these four metals—and I'm not that hot for platinum, by the way—no government can master."

The case for the freedom giving aspects of gold has been concisely summed up in the previously referred to study of "The International Bank Credit Analyst" as follows:

"Money has two basic qualities—store of value and medium of exchange. Lack of one destroys the true quality of an asset. These qualities are imputed by the public to particular assets and are based on trust and confidence. Governments, pathetically thrashing around trying to stop the symptoms of financial trouble, are in no position to dictate what is and what is not money. That is the prerogative of the people, and they have always attributed the money quality to gold in times of great difficulty. Gold can be bought and sold and exchanged for goods and services anywhere in the world in any size with anonymity, no questions asked. No other asset can make a similar claim.

"Central banks, in their choice of reserves, recognize implicitly assets with the soundest money qualities, which explains each's tenacious grip on its existing gold holdings. Each would be delighted to see others sell gold but who is to be first? With the progressive collapse of international financial cooperation and widespread mutual distrust, meaningful gold sales by central banks are most unlikely, since gold represents the ultimate in international sovereignty. The price of gold, then, probably has little to fear from central bank actions in the gold market, other than continued verbal harassment which could have the effect of adding to short run instability and risk."

Perhaps the best single presentation of the case for gold is that presented in a speech before the New York Society Analysts on July 13, 1973, by Miroslav A. Kriz, of the First National City Bank (and previously, from 1945-1958, with the Federal Reserve Bank of New York, and before that with the League of Nations, 1936-1945). Here are some excerpts from that talk:

"Gold remains deeply imbedded in the international monetary system . . . If the Treasury really believed that gold was on its way out as an international money metal, it would be more willing to allow Americans to buy and hold it as an ordinary commodity . . .

"The governments of continental European countries and Japan have, over the past 20 years, tripled their gold stocks . . ."

He points out that the financial powers outside the United States resist demonetization of gold and continue to refrain from selling gold on the international gold market because:
1. Gold is money over which no government

has direct and decisive control, especially since the United States' holdings of monetary gold stocks have diminished from 71% in 1949 to less than 25% of all of the world's monetary gold stocks, while that of other countries has risen.

2. Gold alone is universally acceptable as a means of payment—dollars or SDRs possibly can be "blocked."

3. Gold is a welcome means of diversification of monetary reserves which are otherwise held in dollars, SDRs, and other paper symbols.

4. Gold continues to have intrinsic value.

He points out that there would be many advantages for the United States if the official price of gold were raised to realistic levels:

1. Gold is still the largest international reserve asset possessed by the United States.

2. With gold revalued, there would be an increase in confidence of foreign monetary authorities which hold large amounts of dollars in their central reserves.

3. For technical monetary reasons arising from the absence of any new gold coming into the monetary system because of the low official price, there would probably be a marked increase in the United States balance of payments position.

4. A gold price increase would enable a return to an international gold exchange standard, and it would facilitate a sustainable and credible relationship between United States international assets and liabilities.

5. An important incidental value would be for the United States to receive real value in gold from Russia for what it sells, without increasing

Russia's potential to the detriment of the United States. If Russia paid the United States in gold, this would increase the United States' financial strength.

Advantages of a realistically higher price of gold to the world are seen as follows:

1. Governments would unfreeze their gold stocks and there would be a reduction in uncertainty in international monetary relationships.

2. Restored convertibility of the dollar would restore confidence in its future value and in the international monetary system as a whole.

3. At the right price, newly mined gold would flow into official stocks and contribute to international liquidity.

The alleged drawbacks are reexamined and refuted:

1. A rise in the gold price is not likely to be inflationary. Such a gold price rise would only recognize inflation that has already occurred.

2. The benefit to Russia, South Africa and France, when examined, would not be detrimental to the United States but would probably be advantageous.

3. It is a mistake to think that there will be any loss in the credibility of the dollar because of past reliance on United States promises that the monetary price of gold would never be raised—especially since a currency is not judged by its past history but on its intrinsic strength and current and prospective factors of strength. "In short, the dollar would certainly not die from a rise in the gold price—provided that the rise was generally recognized to be necessary and made to

stick."

4. The philosophical arguments that monetization of gold is unscientific economics and retrogressive politics, and "irrational", are untenable because gold has its own justification, paper money depreciates; and in practical reality, liberating U.S. money and fiscal policy from the constraints of gold has only resulted in the money supply being "expanded relentlessly and, at times, excessively."

5. In reality "the real constraint on monetary and fiscal stimulation is not gold. It is the limit beyond which inflation is unacceptable to the people of the United States—a limit that, most regrettably, has proved much too elastic but that is nevertheless, very real, as conclusively evidenced once again by the current concern of the administration about the political consequences of an inflation."

Mr. Kriz concludes that the worst fear is that the world will be engulfed in inflation. "In such a contingency, gold—it can be confidently predicted—will be catapulted into a position of unchallenged primacy in international payments and reserves . . . Hopefully . . it will become evident that the detente with the East cannot be fruitful if there is monetary and trade warfare within the West . . ."

Further support for this view that gold must be remonetized appeared in an historic editorial entitled "Is it time to return to the gold standard?" of the *Times* of London, written by its editor-in-chief William Rees-Mogg, and which appeaed in its issue of May 1st, 1974. This editorial is all the more important because, previously the *Times* of London had been firmly anti-gold.

Here is a brilliant condensation of Mr. Rees-Mogg's conclusions published in the *International Harry Schultz Letter* #317, end of May issue, 1974 (published by Financial and Economic Research Corporation, address P.O. Box 1161, Basel 4002, Switzerland):

The gold standard is "an option almost un-mentioned among the world's leading central bankers and treasury officials." He speaks of the implications for gold "of a progressive failure of all paper (money systems)." He defines the gold standard as "simply the free convertibility of a currency into gold at a fixed price. No price is eternal, but once a price is fixed, it becomes the chief aim of economic policy to maintain it, not as a fetish but as the axle of an economy. Such an arrangement is to some extent self-regulating a strong currency attracts gold deposits which expand the credit base and increase economic activity, including imports, while a weak currency loses gold with a consequent reduction in the credit base, a rise in interest rates, and a fall in activity and imports."

He lists the national conflicts between short and long term expedience under a managed paper currency situation. For example, when short-term advantage requires a money supply increase, it hurts the long-term effect by increasing prices, and in the still longer run, boosts money supply further and hikes prices and doesn't lower interest rates. In a democracy, with frequent elections, there's always pressure for short-term expediency. Economic management is bent to win elections.

Mr. Rees-Mogg recalls that Montagu Norman (Bank of England Governor) forecasted all in 1925: "Floating exchange rates will be an incentive to governments at times to undertake various types of paper money expedience and inflation . . . after some attempt at some other mechanism for credit and prices regulation, some kind of monetary crisis will finally result in *restoring* gold to its former position, but only after a period of hardship and suffering and possibly some social and political disorder."

Mr. Rees-Mogg cites the price stability under a gold standard. Bread cost 10 pence a loaf in 1820 and 5 pence a loaf in 1895, 75 years later. Interest rates, he notes, were 4½% in 1823, 3% in 1910, yet there was a rise in real standards (of living), as money wages index was 110 in 1920 and 181 in 1906. Mr. Rees-Mogg says: "Since the dollar ceased to be convertible into gold, a period still only 2½ years, the world itself has been taken off the gold standard (in any form). The results are already apparent and they are disastrous . . . World inflation, a disease of world (paper) currencies, has immensely accelerated. Hardship and suffering have already occurred, and *social* and *political disorder* may not be far behind . . .

"Yet there's been no inflation in prices expressed in terms of gold, if one treats gold as the only non-managed world currency. Since convertibility ended, gold has risen from $43 to $175. Thus the dollar has fallen by 75%." He says your house may be worth twice what it was three years ago, but it's worth the *same* number of ounces of gold.

Same with oil. "At a time of extreme currency inflation, gold has quietly provided what money is for, a stable medium of exchange and standard of value . . .

"Gold works, but paper, unless based ultimately on gold does not. Gold is real money and paper is pretend money . . . Paper money is only as good as the men who control it and they're under consistent pressure to print more. Gold exists in limited quantity and added to in limited and predictable quantity. Paper money's value is precisely the value of the politician's promise . . . Gold's value is protected by the inability of politicians to manufacture it. In any system the base has a credit superstructure, multiplying its purchase-power. But a gold base imposes its own discipline on credit, a paper base is capable of unlimited (growth). Inflation is limited only when men believe there's no more money to be had. With paper money that belief is unattainable."

He cites arguments against gold that South Africa and U.S.S.R. may benefit. Says it's a weak argument. Besides, "the free market is *already* providing these high prices." You can't concede ground already lost in battle. Even so, he adds: Greater wealth won't make these nations less tolerable to us. In fact a bit more prosperity might aid peaceable elements in the Soviet Union and also the blacks in South Africa. In any case, he concludes, "it's absurd to compare the small benefit to these two nations, of a higher gold price (which already exists anyway) with a greater benefit to world communism gained by a total inflationary collapse of our paper currencies."

He cites numerous benefits from a gold standard: lower mortgage rates, house price stability, more housing brought onto the market, low bank rates, more stimulation to business, less currency speculation and fluctuation, discipline on balance of payments, etc. Says: "If gold were fixed at 100 an ounce ($245) and the currency reorganized so that a new one pound gold note replaced ten pounds of old notes, the new one pound would have a gold equivalent of one/tenth of an ounce."

Because of its size, he goes on to say, the United States is at the center of the decaying currency system. Until the center falls, the outer nations may be propped up. The *decisive* crisis *may* not come till after the next cycle of recession and boom; it's unpredictable. But when the center falls, everyone will go down with it, in varying degrees. "Events will destroy the floating paper system. The refusal of oil producing nations to accept depreciating paper currencies at the old rate shows what happens to a currency system that can't command confidence. . . . When the paper system collapses, the survivors will dig in the rubble and they will find gold."

As this is being written, the power of gold has begun to emerge triumphant. At the meeting of the International Monetary Fund's Committee of Twenty, at Washington on June 12, 13 and 14, 1974, gold was brought back to life in the international monetary system by the adoption of an agreement to permit nations to use their gold reserves as collateral for loans, pricing the gold realistically at a market-related price. Here is how the scheme is to work, as reported by the *Wall Street Journal* issue of June 13, 1974:

"Washington—The major industrial nations agreed on a plan to let economically distressed countries expand their borrowing power by using official gold stocks as security for international loans.

"The agreement by finance ministers of the so-called Group of 10 industrial nations could be of major benefit to such nations as Italy and France, which have already stretched their borrowing power to finance international payments deficits and might have difficulty raising additional money without the new gold-as-collateral arrangement.

"While nothing legally prevented a nation from using gold as collateral before, it wasn't economically practical because of the metal's two-price system. With the free market price of gold near $156 an ounce, no nation was willing to risk its gold as loan collateral at the 'official' price of $42.22 an ounce. The new agreement, in effect, could nearly quadruple the value of gold as collateral by permitting the lender—most likely a central bank—to value the pledged metal at a price much closer to the free-market quote than to the official level.

"The gold agreement, reached late Tuesday night and announced yesterday by the U.S. Treasury, overshadowed other developments as the free world's finance ministers and central bankers met to act on a series of interim actions to revise the international monetary system. In yesterday's meeting of the International Monetary Fund's Committee of 20, the authorities approved with unexpected speed a number of these steps, including new guidelines governing 'floating' currency values and a new scheme to define and value Special Drawing Rights, the IMF's brand of international money.

A Compromise Agreement:
"The agreement on gold represented a compromise that met the desires of some European nations to make their gold stocks more useful in coping with international payments deficits . . ."

Gold has emerged victorious already as evidenced by the recent agreement by Germany to lend $2 billion to Italy, secured by gold. The real effect of this agreement in remonetizing gold is fully explained in a news article in the *New York Times*, September 2, 1974, under the by-line of John M. Lee, as follows:

"The evaluation of gold at a price higher than the official $42.22 an ounce in the new loan agreement between West Germany and Italy is regarded by economic observers as a revival of the use of gold in the battered world monetary system.

"Such a development runs counter to avowed United States policy which has attempted to demonetize gold—that is, diminish its importance in international monetary transactions.

"The loan agreement, announced Saturday, calls for West Germany to extend a $2 billion credit to Italy to help her avert national bankruptcy from a huge trade deficit brought on by high-priced oil imports and the costs of servicing large international debts.

"One of the key provisions is that Italy will pledge an undisclosed portion of her substantial gold reserves as collateral. But the gold will be valued at 80 per cent of the free-market price for gold during the last eight weeks. In this period, the price of gold has ranged from $145 to $156.

"The value of gold for the purpose of this agreement between governments is thus about $120. Gold has never been valued so high for monetary purposes.

"In recent years Washington has initiated or supported various moves intended to trivialize the part gold has traditionally played in international commerce.

"These moves include the creation of a new official reserve asset, Special Drawing Rights, or "paper gold," in 1968, the cutting of the official link between gold and the dollar in 1971 and the enactment of a law this year permitting American citizens to buy and hold gold.

"However, the American campaign received a setback at the beginning of the summer when the ten leading financial powers, the so-called Group of Ten, agreed that countries using their official gold reserves as collateral for loans might agree with lenders on a value for their gold at a price much closer to the market price.

"The official price of gold (the price at which gold is valued in transactions between national goverments) has been $42.22 an ounce since February 1973. But the price in the free market has ranged up to $180 an ounce.

"Although the Group of Ten decision was described as having general applicability, it was apparent that Italy was intended to be the chief beneficiary.

"Following the summit meeting at Bellagio, between President Mariano Rumor of Italy and Chancellor Helmut Schmidt of West Germany, Italy is, in effect, issuing gold-backed promisory notes based on a higher gold price.

"Other nations, hard pressed financially by oil import costs, might follow suit. In the past, a higher price for gold has been associated with a lower value for the United States dollar. However, the dollar has been floating free of any fixed value since early last year."

Chapter VIII

Some Facts About Gold

The discovery of gold and its utilization is lost in antiquity. The earliest indication of man's use of gold goes back to about 4000 B.C. (6,000 years ago) when gold dust and nuggets at the edge of the Nile drew attention by their beauty, weight and softness. These qualities, together with its scarcity, made the yellow, easily workable metal desirable for ornaments—rings, bracelets, earrings, headpieces and breastplates—objects all familiar to anyone who has seen a collection of Egyptian antiquities.

As trade developed in the ancient world (and there was more commerce in those ancient times than we commonly realize) gold began to take on importance as an object for exchanging values, and thereby added flexibility to the usual clumsy system of bartering bulky goods. By 3400 B.C. gold had been found so useful to traders that a very early Egyptian king, Menes, had gold bars officially produced with a uniform weight of about 14 grams (less than ½ ounce) stamped with his name. The first gold coins appear to have been invented by King Croesus of Lydia (died 546 B.C.). He stamped out round silver and gold coins with his picture on them, of uniform quality and size which gained acceptance in trade all over the ancient world. The Persians later conquered Lydia, seized its gold, and minted their own coins called the "daric" which became internationally accepted. Then Alexander conquered Persia, issued his own coins, and from then on gold coinage was established in history as money.

Gold has many unusual qualities. It is so ductile that one grain, about 1/500th of an ounce, can be drawn into a 500 foot wire. It is so malleable that one grain can be beaten into gold leaf to cover 56 square inches—1/281,980th of an inch thick. It is unaffected by water and air at any temperature, so it is tarnish proof. While it can be dissolved in a mixture of nitric and hydrochloric acids (the *aqua regia* of the alchemists) it is unaffected by other acids or alkalis alone. Because of this remarkable durability, it is believed that 90% of all gold ever mined is still in use today.

While gold is rare, it has been found all over the world in land and in the sea. Egypt was the chief source of gold in ancient times, but it was also produced in significant quantities in India, Tashkent, around the Black Sea, the Arabian Peninsula, Greece and Dacia (now Romania). After 700 B.C. Spain was a major producer. Then, in succession, gold was found in South America when conquered by the Spaniards, Russia discovered gold in the Urals; the United States in California, Alaska and Nevada. Gold was found in Australia in 1850 and a few years later in New Zealand. The most extensive gold ores are those of South Africa which were first discovered in 1868. They remain by far the largest producers today.

Gold is commonly measured in troy ounces. One kilogram of gold equals 32.151 troy ounces, or, 1 troy ounce of gold equals a little more than 31 grams.

South Africa is much the largest gold producer in the world, supplying approximately 75% of the total world production each year. In 1973, South Africa produced 852 metric tons of gold out of a total output by non-Communist countries of 1,119 tons. In addition Russia produces some significant amount of gold, but this is kept secret. From time to time, Russia sells gold in the West to pay for food and other goods needed from the West. It is estimated that Russia sold 60 tons in 1971, 220 tons in 1972, and 275 tons in 1973. It is believed that Russia sells gold only when pressed by great necessity.

What happens to the large quantity of gold that is produced every year? The answer to this question tells us that even more than being a medium of exchange or a store of value, gold is a commodity. It is a commercial product like copper, coffee or cotton. In fact, the consumption of gold over the past few years has increased at the rate of about 4% per year.

The two main uses to which gold is put are manufacturing and investment. The chief industrial demand for gold is the jewelry trade which takes 70% of all new production. About 20% of new gold coming to market is used by industry in electronic equipment, dentistry, plating, medallions, and a variety of other uses such as fountain pens and gold leaf for decoration.

The remaining 10% is accounted for by investment (using the term broadly to including hoarding and speculation).

The investment demand for gold should not be underestimated. Hoarding of gold and silver is deeply rooted in a large part of the world's population, not only because of age-old tradition which looks upon gold as a store of value, but because in most of the world people have few other facilities such as bank accounts or securities in which to store their savings. The trend for individuals to use gold as a hedge against monetary turmoil and potential disaster has been increasing in recent years even in the United States as witnessed by the advertisements of coin and silver bullion dealers. Furthermore, it may be that some countries continue to buy gold to add to their monetary reserves, as it is believed France is doing.

In an editorial in the *Wall Street Journal*, June 21, 1974 issue, reference is made to testimony before the Senate and House Banking Committees by Charles Stahl, publisher of *Green's Market Commodity Comments*. Mr. Stahl has been testifying for years asking those committees to consider the possibility that a large part of the United States balance-of-payments deficit is due to illegal purchases of gold by Americans abroad. He estimates that 1972 illegal American gold holdings abroad amounted to $6 billion; in 1973, $13 billion; today, about $20 to $24 billion.

With demand growing at the rate of 4% a year and likely to be increased because of the growing population of the world, the increasing prosperity and industrialization of the underdeveloped countries and many other factors, we must ask: What about the supply? A study of world gold production shows that (excluding the unknowable but relatively small Russian output) new gold supplied by free world producers peaked at 1,273 tons in 1970, declined in 1971, continued declining in 1972 and 1973, in which year the new supply was 1,119 tons.

A study by Merrill, Lynch, Pierce, Fenner and Smith, Inc., reports that the situation has continued to deteriorate in 1974 and that the lower trend of production may be expected to continue in the future. This is due to two basic factors: The exhaustion of richer ores and the increasing costs of the labor and materials required for production.

This brief review of supply and demand factors only augurs for a firm support of a high and increasing gold price.

That view is further supported by a mid-year (July 1974) report of Consolidated Gold Fields Limited which says that the rush for gold due to inflation and the movement of investors away from securities, real estate and other investments resulted in hoarders and speculators buying 508 tons of gold—about half of the total annual output by free world countries. The report also confirmed the continuation of the decline in new production which began in 1970. These late figures show that

South Africa produced 852 tons in 1973 as against 908 in 1972 (the Soviet production was estimated at 370 tons in 1973).

The report further notes that the increase in hoarding was the greatest for any year since 1968 when the free market in gold under the two-tier system first began to operate. Sizable purchasers were in France, West Germany, Switzerland, Latin America, Canada, Indonesia, Taiwan, and Hong Kong. It was believed, also, that there were sizeable purchases by Americans through "off-shore funds."

The Consolidated Gold Fields report also said that future demands are hard to evaluate but it predicted that continuing inflation would increase the investment demand for gold.

Chapter IX

Available Gold and Gold Related Investments

For the investor in gold mining stocks, there are really only two areas providing investment opportunities: namely, North America (Canada and the United States) and South Africa. The nature of the gold deposits is very different in these two areas and thus provides different factors for consideration when making investment decisions.

In Canada and the United States gold appears in quartz veins and the geological structures are of a complexity that makes it difficult to estimate reserves beyond those immediately and clearly proven. While many mines probably have extensive reserves they are difficult to assess and this situation gives rise to a large speculative factor in trying to evaluate them.

In South Africa, on the other hand, the geological character of the gold bearing ores are unique, because gold is found in conglomerated formations which are exceptionally continuous so that their extent can be more easily determined and, further, lends itself to modern techniques for their exploitation and development.

Thus, a major area of investment is in South African gold mining stocks. These may be divided into categories as follows:

I. South African mining companies (of which there are about 40). These can be subdivided into four types:
   a. long-life mines
   b. medium-life mines
   c. short-life or speculative mines
   d. the mining finance companies

II. North American companies can be divided into:
   a. United States mines mainly in gold production.
   b. United States mines which are large gold producers whose main activities are not gold mining.
   c. Speculative mines
   d. Canadian mines mainly in gold production but of a speculative nature.

III. Investment trusts divided into:
   a. Open-end or mutual fund
   b. Closed-end

IV. Investment in gold—the metal itself, divided into:
   a. gold bullion
   b. gold coins and medallions which have numismatic value.
   c. gold coins—for the gold itself
   d. fine gold jewelry
   e. coarse gold jewelry

V. Futures Markets.

Each of these categories will be considered in the following chapters.

Investment Strategies: Metal vs. Paper

If investors wish to own some gold for its "insurance" characteristics, they will assess the wisdom of owning proxies—notably South African gold-mining securities—very differently. Many will not wish to own pieces of paper which may embody many of the very risks they are seeking to avoid in the first place: political, mining, cost inflation, interest rate, equity, and exchange risks. Changes in any of these can cause the share prices to diverge from moving parallel with the metal.

Our updated table tracing these divergences (please see page 15) shows that *a remarkable improvement in the relative performance of the South African shares took place in 1979.*

The reasons for the new and more favorable perception of the risks of holding South African paper are discussed in Chapter X. Suffice it to note here that, when dividends are included, the South African share performance approximately paralleled the performance of bullion itself in 1979 (+ 131.9%), in sharp contrast to experience after 1975.

In fact, the performance of the shares outside South Africa (+ 89.2% in 1979), relative to the movement of the shares within the Republic (+

108.9%) is even better than indicated in the table. This is because the Financial Times gold index reflects the strength of sterling and the consequent decline in the dollar premium lowered the returns on non-British securities owned by U.K. investors. During 1979 exchange controls were abolished in the U.K., and the dollar premium actually disappeared.

These developments have been reflected in the sharp contraction of the discount on the financial rand. (For an explanation of the financial rand, please see the footnote below).

In brief, U.S. shareholders in South African shares during 1979 benefited not only from the movement in the price of gold *and* the underlying shares, but also from a decline of the discount on the financial rand from 44% at the end of 1978 to 27% at year-end in 1979.

GOLD: METAL VS. PAPER 1974-1979

(a) Securities Rand represent a pool of blocked (not freely transferable South African Rand. They may be purchased only by foreigners, and may be used only for investment within South Africa. Their value, determined by supply and demand, is currently around $0.99, compared with the official parity of R1=$1.22. The discount is a measure of foreigners' perception of the political and investment risk in South Africa. It is thus currently around 19%, compared with 42% at the beginning of 1979.

GOLD: METAL VS. PAPER 1974-1979

	Gold Bullion London (Aft. Fixing) (U.S. $)	Indices South African Mines	
		London FT Gold	Johannesburg Gold
Year-End 1974	$187.50	354	386
Year-End 1975	140.25	238	218
1976			
High	140.35	247	227
Low	103.50	79	113
Year-End	134.50	122	171
1977			
High	167.50	175	215
Low	129.00	95	139
Year-End	164.95	133	205
1978			
High	242.75	207	272
Low	165.70	124	186
Year-End	226.00	142	254
1979			
End-January	232.38	165	270
End-February	251.63	177	279
End-March	240.10	155	267
End-April	245.30	150	256
End-May	274.60	196	291
End-June	277.60	168	295
End-July	296.45	152	296
End-August	315.10	174	336
End-September	397.25	250	412
End-October	382.00	202	308
End-November	415.65	234	423
End-December	524.00	269	531
High	524.00	269	531
Low	232.38	150	256
1980			
January 23	695.00	311.6	538
% Change End-1979 Relative to:			
End-1974	179.5%	(24.0)%	37.6%
End-1975	273.6	13.0	143.6
End-1976	389.6	120.5	210.5
End-1977	217.7	102.3	159.0
End-1978	131.9	89.4	109.1
% Change January-23 Relative to:			
End-1978	207.5	119.4	111.8
End-1979	32.6	15.8	1.3

Official Rand	Securities Rand (a)	Securities Rand (a) Discount	Dow Jones Spot Commodities Index	
1.45	0.965	33.5%	385	
1.15	1.035	10.0	296	
1.15	1.025	10.9	386	
1.15	0.640	44.3	294	
1.15	0.665	42.2	371	U.S. $/S.A. Rand Exchange Rate
1.15	0.855	25.7	449	
1.15	0.655	43.0	342	
1.15	0.725	37.0	342	
1.15	0.840	27.0	402	
1.15	0.638	44.5	344	
1.15	0.650	43.5	385	
1.152	0.665	42.0	376	
1.181	0.685	42.0	387	
1.183	0.755	34.0	378	
1.179	0.775	34.0	389	
1.185	0.893	25.0	392	
1.185	0.880	26.0	424	
1.194	0.853	30.0	399	
1.198	0.883	26.0	403	
1.210	0.893	26.0	416	
1.208	0.813	33.0	400	
1.204	0.863	28.0	419	
1.210	0.881	27.0	419	
1.181	0.685	42.0	424	
1.185	0.893	25.0	376	
1.223	0.99	19.0	437	
(16.6)%	(8.7)%	-	8.8%	
5.2	(14.9)	-	41.6	
5.2	32.5	-	12.9	
5.2	21.5	-	22.5	
5.2	35.5	-	8.8	
6.3	52.3	-	13.5	
1.1	12.4	-	4.3	

MKT. PRICE	MONTH	UNIT COST DOLLAR COST	AVERAGE AVERAGE
$200/oz.	1	1.00 oz./$200 = 200	1 @ $200 = $200
$300/oz.	2	.666 oz./$200 = 200	1 @ $300 = $300
$400/oz.	3	.500 oz./$200 = 200	1 @ $400 = $400
$600/oz.	4	.333 oz./$200 = 200	1 @ $600 = $600
$800/oz.	5	.250 oz./$200 = 200	1 @ $800 = $800
$700/oz.	6	.286 oz./$200 = 200	1 @ $700 = $700
$600/oz.	7	.333 oz./$200 = 200	1 @ $600 = $600
$500/oz.	8	.400 oz./$200 = 200	1 @ $500 = $500
$600/oz.	9	.333 oz./$200 = 200	1 @ $600 = $600
$700/oz.	10	.286 oz./$200 = 200	1 @ $700 = $700

| $540 | 4.387 | 2000 2000 | 10 oz. 5400 5400 |

average cost of gold for 10 months— $540

average price per oz.— $455.89

average price per oz.— $540

* dollar cost averaging works best while systematically buying in an upward trending market that has normal up & down price fluctuations. Unit cost averaging out performs DCA when the price runs up with few price setbacks.

Chapter X
New Perspective On
Investing in South Africa

Despite ever-present short-term risk, I believe that an important fundamental positive change has, is, and will continue to take place in the long-term investor perception of political risk of investing in South Africa.

Since investors seek a gold exposure as a method of preserving capital in real terms, it would be irresponsible to deny that there exists risk both in the gold price, and in holding gold shares. This remains particularly true in the case of South African gold mining securities in view of the socio-political risks. If the metal reacts, and/or disturbances erupt in South Africa, in the short-run the share prices are likely, as in the past, to respond at least as, and probably even more negatively than, bullion itself.

Why, then, are we more positive about the longer-term changes in attitude? We would summarize our reasons as follows:

1. *Rapid changes are taking place within South Africa society itself.* Everybody loves a whipping-boy, and South Africa, with its absurd and immoral doctrine of apartheid, proved an easy target all critics could agree about. However, the charges are being levelled at facts that are increasingly out-of-date: South African society appears to be in the midst of major radical change.

   Pieter G. Koornhof, South Africa's Minister of Cooperation and Development and the man responsible for administering laws concerning blacks, has stated, "A society where any man, whatever his creed or color, is denied human rights, is an unjust one. I am fully aware of this and so is my Government. We are doing something about it every day. We will not rest until racial discrimination has disappeared from our statute books and everyday life in South Africa. In saying this I have the full support of my Prime Minister. Recently, the Wiehahn Commission recommended, and the South African Government accepted, far-reaching measures to insure equal pay for work of equal value for everybody, nondiscrimination in jobs and facilities, and black trade unionism. At the same time, the Riekert Commission suggested sweeping reforms of our labor system aimed at ending racial discrimination and improving the day-to-day living of the urban black in South Africa. Once again, we are not only listening to such advice but acting accordingly."

2. *Moves toward settling problems in Rhodesia (Zimbabwe), and South-West Africa (Namibia)* should accelerate movement towards a defusion of tension throughout southern Africa.

3. *South Africa is the most powerful economy on the African Continent.* With 4% of its total area and 6% of its population, it accounts for 25% of total GNP and over 50% of its generated electricity. It is its only net food exporter. In brief, it cannot be easily ignored. Nor is it, least of all in private by many states which castigate it in public. A flourishing and growing trade exists with 19 African states which nominally maintain sanctions against it. An economic, hydroelectric, and transportation infrastructure has developed that has forged strong links with other states in southern Africa, including Angola, South-West Africa, Mozambique, Rhodesia and Zambia. South Africans run the railways and ports in Mozambique. Malawis are again working on the mines. Following the decline of Mozambican mineworkers from 91,356 in 1975 to 35,000 at present, and consequent drop in "deferred payment" remittances from R40.2 million in 1976 to R24.4 million in 1977, the government of Mozambique requested the Chamber of Mines to step up its recruiting of Mozambican workers.

The gold/minerals boom appears likely to strengthen the economy even further.

South Africa achieved a record annualized surplus on the current account of its balance of payments in the third quarter of 1979 of $4 billion, more than twice the year-earlier figure. External debt has been reduced through large loan repayments. According to the Stellenbosch Bureau of Economic Research, real growth is placed at 4% in 1980, compared with 3.1% in 1979, while inflation is estimated to recede to 11.5% from 13% in 1979.

4. *South Africa is less vulnerable to higher oil prices than is commonly supposed.* Well-endowed with large coal and hydroelectric energy, oil represents 23% of the Republic's energy consumption. While it must import 95% of such oil, the existing SASOL oil-from-coal plant provides 5%. Expansion of a "SASOL-2" in December 1980 will raise this domestic supply to 30%, and of a "SASOL-3" to 47-50% by 1983. Existing strategic reserves have been estimated at 2-3 years' demand.

5. *South Africa stands to benefit from the belated Western awakening to the Russian/Cuban/surrogate threat in Africa.* Since 1975, 40,000 Cuban and other Russian mercenaries have been rampaging across the Continent, from Angola through Mozambique, Ethiopia, Somalia and Eritrea. Across the Red Sea, they are active in North and South Yemen. The Russian invasion of Afghanistan and manipulation of Iran has finally

awakened awareness of their strategic designs, via Baluchistan, on the Gulf, from which 60-70% of the OECD's oil flows. (In addition, the OECD estimates that Russia's Eastern European satellites will be totally dependent on foreign oil by 1985, while Russia itself would become a net importer of oil by the end of the decade.) The Cape sea route is a critical link in the transportation chain. South Africa itself possesses 7 out of 15 African ports south of the Equator.

6. *South Africa's role as an absolutely essential source of strategic minerals has been very considerably enhanced by the new-found realization that the Russians are not Boy Scouts.* The combination of South African and Russian supplies for a large number of minerals essential if Western industry is not to literally grind to a halt and military security to be affected, expressed as a percentage of the world total, is high. A reduction of East-West trade following the Russian invasion of Afghanistan, while it would not halt the flow of Russian exports, enhances the importance and value of South Africa's proven and reliable old-established network of trading links.

In brief, it appears that the tendency for conducting Western foreign policy with references to debates in the United Nations may be gone, if not forever, at least for a long time.

The tables on the following three pages illustrates the combined South African and Russian percentage of key minerals with respect to world reserves, production and exports.

THERE ARE MANY COMPANIES AND SECURITIES MENTIONED, REFERRED TO, OR BRIEFLY DESCRIBED IN THIS BOOK. INFORMATION RESPECTING THEM WAS TAKEN FROM SOURCES CONSIDERED RELIABLE BUT IN NO WAY GUARANTEED. MOREOVER, THE DATA CONCERNING ANY INDIVIDUAL ISSUE WAS NECESSARILY PREPARED SOME MONTHS AGO, AND CONSEQUENTLY IS OUTDATED. ACCORDINGLY, IF THE READER IS INTERESTED IN ANY OF THE SECURITIES MENTIONED FOR POSSIBLE PURCHASE, SALE OR RETENTION, IT IS ESSENTIAL THAT HE OR SHE ACQUIRE THE LATEST AND MOST AUTHORITATIVE INFORMATION ABOUT IT BEFORE MAKING ANY INVESTMENT DECISION. THIS INFORMATION SHOULD BE SECURED FROM THE COMPANY OR A RESPONSIBLE BROKER, DEALER, INVESTMENT ADVISOR, FINANCIAL PUBLICATION, OR SERVICE. IN NO EVENT IS ANY RECOMMENDATION OR ENDORSEMENT OF ANY SECURITY MADE OR IMPLIED; AND NOTHING HEREIN IS TO BE CONSIDERED UNDER ANY CIRCUMSTANCES AS AN OFFER OR INDUCEMENT TO BUY, SELL, OR HOLD ANY SECURITY AT ANY TIME.

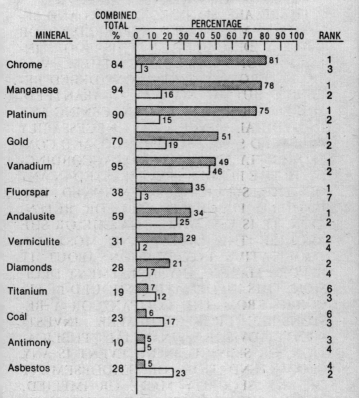

**THE ROLE OF SOUTH AFRICA AND THE U.S.S.R.
IN WORLD MINERAL RESERVES - 1978**

MINERAL	COMBINED TOTAL %	PERCENTAGE	RANK
Chrome	84	81 / 3	1 / 3
Manganese	94	78 / 16	1 / 2
Platinum	90	75 / 15	1 / 2
Gold	70	51 / 19	1 / 2
Vanadium	95	49 / 46	1 / 2
Fluorspar	38	35 / 3	1 / 7
Andalusite	59	34 / 25	1 / 2
Vermiculite	31	29 / 2	2 / 4
Diamonds	28	21 / 7	2 / 4
Titanium	19	7 / 12	6 / 3
Coal	23	6 / 17	6 / 3
Antimony	10	5 / 5	3 / 4
Asbestos	28	5 / 23	4 / 2

▨ South Africa
☐ U.S.S.R.

SOURCES: Mineral Bureau of South
Africa and U.S. Bureau of
Mines

Drexel Burnham Lambert
INCORPORATED

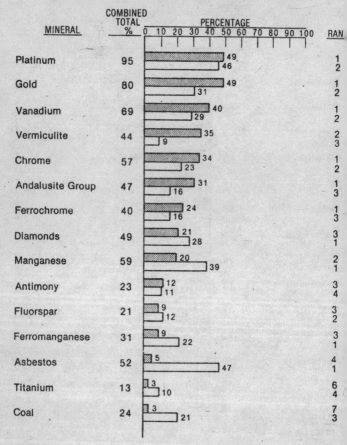

THE ROLE OF SOUTH AFRICA AND THE U.S.S.R. IN WORLD MINERAL PRODUCTION - 1978

MINERAL	COMBINED TOTAL %	PERCENTAGE (South Africa / U.S.S.R.)	RANK
Platinum	95	49 / 46	1 / 2
Gold	80	49 / 31	1 / 2
Vanadium	69	40 / 29	1 / 2
Vermiculite	44	35 / 9	2 / 3
Chrome	57	34 / 23	1 / 2
Andalusite Group	47	31 / 16	1 / 3
Ferrochrome	40	24 / 16	1 / 3
Diamonds	49	21 / 28	3 / 1
Manganese	59	20 / 39	2 / 1
Antimony	23	12 / 11	3 / 4
Fluorspar	21	9 / 12	3 / 2
Ferromanganese	31	9 / 22	3 / 1
Asbestos	52	5 / 47	4 / 1
Titanium	13	3 / 10	6 / 4
Coal	24	3 / 21	7 / 3

South Africa
U.S.S.R.

SOURCES: Mineral Bureau of South Africa and U.S. Bureau of Mines

Drexel Burnham Lambert
INCORPORATED

TABLE 10

THE ROLE OF SOUTH AFRICA AND THE U.S.S.R. IN WORLD MINERAL EXPORTS - 1978

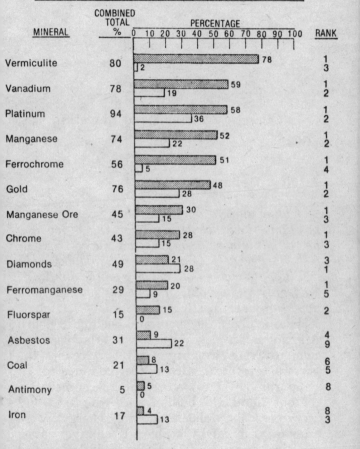

MINERAL	COMBINED TOTAL %	PERCENTAGE (South Africa / U.S.S.R.)	RANK
Vermiculite	80	78 / 2	1 / 3
Vanadium	78	59 / 19	1 / 2
Platinum	94	58 / 36	1 / 2
Manganese	74	52 / 22	1 / 2
Ferrochrome	56	51 / 5	1 / 4
Gold	76	48 / 28	1 / 2
Manganese Ore	45	30 / 15	1 / 3
Chrome	43	28 / 15	1 / 3
Diamonds	49	21 / 28	3 / 1
Ferromanganese	29	20 / 9	1 / 5
Fluorspar	15	15 / 0	2
Asbestos	31	9 / 22	4 / 9
Coal	21	8 / 13	6 / 5
Antimony	5	5 / 0	8
Iron	17	4 / 13	8 / 3

▨ South Africa
☐ U.S.S.R.

SOURCES: Mineral Bureau of South
Africa and U.S. Bureau of
Mines

Chapter XI

Changing Dynamics of Investing in Mining Shares

A. New Dynamics

I have always advocated that, except for core positions, the South African shares should seldom be bought and held, but instead traded. We now feel that recent developments have rendered the traditional strategy of "trading on the dividend" not only inappropriate but misguided and potentially very costly.

Historically, analysis of and trading in South African mining securities was complex but comparatively straightforward. For decades, the players operated within the confines of a comparatively known and static environment. On the one hand, the bullion price was fixed and known. Costs (labor, material, energy) were known and fairly stable. Exchange rates, affecting import costs, were fixed. Inflation and interest rates were low and predictable. The other major piece in the equation was determining grade, the mines being constrained by law under the terms of their leases to mill to the average grade in order to prolong the life of the industry — and this was seldom difficult in one of the documented industries in the world. Finally, the mines, as classic wasting assets, paid out virtually the totality of their earnings after mine taxes, lease payments, *and capital expenditures,* in the form of dividends, the latter being regarded as returns *of* capital rather than returns *on* capital.

Historically, therefore, it has been a comparatively simple standard operating procedure both for the mining finance houses which manage the mines and for specialist analysts to factor in these data into their computers, estimate dividends, and trade the shares on this basis. The process involved both maximizing returns by taking advantage of yield differentials, and "trading on the dividend"—i.e. buying shares prior to and disposing of them following dividend disbursement.

This straightforward approach has been profoundly altered by the dynamic changes which now characterize the gold share market. *To continue to play this simplistic game without a proper understanding of these changes, in our opinion, involves enormous financial risk.* The risk is particularly applicable to those who have been successfully invested in South African shares over the past year. The uninitiated newcomers may come to believe that their unquestioned success was primarily due to their trading capabilities. In fact, of course, the table on page 124 shows that virtually *any* exposure to the gold share market in 1979-80 would have resulted in excellent returns (though still *smaller* than returns on bullion). With the metal soaring by 308%, the relevance of dividend returns, *in the short run* was, to put it charitably, tangential. This is particularly important when so many of the ingredients in the equation are subject to very rapid change: bullion price rose by 132% and oil costs by more than 60% in 1979 alone, while black and white labor costs advanced by 535% and 130%, respectively, during the six-and-a-half years through mid-1979. In addition it is necessary to factor in fluctuations in interest rates and exchange rates.

Historical experience strongly suggests that the one constant which gold investors must anticipate is the unexpected. We have alluded to some of the possible forces which could threaten the gold price. It is an illusion to suppose that if any of them materialize the shares would not stage a substantial retreat. In addition, there do exist short-term political risks affecting the shares themselves.

To illustrate the impact of cost escalation: Mr. Dennis Etheridge, president of South Africa's Chamber of Mines and head of Anglo-American Corporation's gold division, stated that ore bodies which were reckoned to be uneconomic to mine 2-3 years ago when the bullion price was well under $200 per ounce were uneconomic at $400 an ounce.

Finally, the surge in mine profits has given many mine managements an opportunity to expand capital expenditures, making for unexpected shocks. As the Financial Mail wrote on December 14, 1979, "On publication of the Gold Fields of South Africa (mining finance group) gold dividends, one broker's immediate reaction was to ask whether there had not been a misprint in his morning paper."

There had not. The dividend announcements were far below expectations. The truth is that when the gold price tide surges from an average per ounce of $194 in 1978 to $304 in 1979 and over $800 in early 1980, it lifts a lot of little boats with it. This is fine, except for those captains under the illusion that they were responsible for the move. These risk painful shock when the tide turns.

Moreover, marketability can become a problem. It should be borne in mind that the total market capitalization of all the South African gold producers *combined* amounts to less than 38% of the market capitalization of IBM. The effective floating supply can be significantly smaller still, because the mining finance houses and institutional investors own substantial blocks.

This is why for several years we have advocated that a gold exposure be an integral part of a carefully-considered *overall* portfolio strategy, including U.S. stocks, bonds and foreign securities, that the subjectively-determined percentage exposure be broken down as follows in order to provide "a hedge within a hedge":

South African shares:	40%
North American shares:	5%
French gold-indexed shares:	5%

Bullion—preferably Krugerrand:	<u>50%</u>
Total	100%

It is *only* within this context that we consider—indeed advocate—exposure to gold mining securities and fold in dividend considerations.

Dividends on several South African shares, including details of ADR payment schedules and estimated dividends at three different gold prices, are included in Appendix I starting on page 135.

In addition:

Appendix II shows the estimated next two ADR dividend payments.

Appendix III shows the actual ADR dividend schedule of 1979.

Appendix IV shows the up-to-date dividend schedule for 1980.

A word of caution when assessing the shares' estimated dividends on the basis of various higher gold prices. The constraint that South African mines "mill to the average grade of the ore" obviously does not mean that mines will shift production with every flutter in the gold price. Physical and cost constraints play an important role, and differ from mine to mine. So does *timing;* the cost of shifting equipment and preparing different shafts can be very high, and mine managements must become convinced that a given price level will prevail for a while. On balance, then, it typically requires from 6 to 18 months to shift grade.

B. Recent Developments

During the June 1979 quarter a number of mines which were able to lower their grade, but this was partially offset by higher mill throughput. With average grade at 8.37 grams per ton vs. 8.35 in the March quarter, total production actually increased to 177,935.5 kilograms. By the September quarter, however, the lowering of grade became more pronounced at 8.12 grams per ton, although, again, an increase in throughput permitted production to increase to 177,995 kilograms.

Increases in working costs have been well maintained in view of higher oil prices, and are placed at 15% for the year as a whole. This compares with a 13.7% increase in 1978, the lowest level in 5 years.

Indications point to a strong December quarter. Production probably dropped by 2.5%, but, with a gold price approaching $400 during the quarter revenues should have increased by at least 20%. Assuming costs rose at a somewhat lesser rate than the 7% during the September quarter, distributable profits may be up by some 30% during the period.

C. U.S. Ownership of South African Mining Shares

There has been an accumulation of the shares in the United States in recent years. The following shows the *approximate* percentage of the capitalization held in the U.S. for a number of leading gold producers, and mining finance houses:

TABLE 11

South African Gold Shares

Blyvooruitzicht	50.0%
Durban Deep	43.5
East Driefontein	16.9
East Rand Gold & Uranium	7.4
East Rand Proprietary Mines	12.6
Free State Geduld	47.3
Hartebeestfontein	23.0
Leslie	14.6
Loraine	36.6
Randfontein	17.9
Southvaal	17.0
Welkom	37.7
Western Deep Levels	32.9
Western Holdings	35.2
Zandpan	3.8

Mining Finance Houses

Anglo American	15.6
Amgold	15.6
DeBeers	10.8

D. Recommended Gold-Related Strategy

In the first place, we continue to be committed to the virtues of maintaining a gold-related position in portfolios. The exact proportion must be a function of each individual investor's or portfolio manager's subjective assessment of the outlook for real rates of return on alternative investment media. In other words, each must determine whether and to what extent he believes that factors are at work which will enhance or reduce real rates of return on stocks, bonds, real estate, etc. Since such factors encompass expectations of future inflation, taxation, political and other uncertainties, there cannot be a "correct" gold-related position; it will always be a fluctuating individual anxiety barometer.

Secondly, aside from fanatical gold bugs, nobody wants gold for its own sake—it is a sterile investment in a rational world.

Third, it would be senseless to purchase gold-related investments as insurance against risk, only to concentrate such insurance in paper mining shares that may embody many of the risks one is seeking to avoid in the first place—political, taxation, currency, mining, market, and so forth.

Therefore, bearing in mind our caveats about subjectivity, we suggest a breakdown among gold-related investments along the following lines:

1. 40% South African gold mining securities, distributed along the lines outlined below;
2. 5% high quality North American gold mining securities—*Dome Mines* ($57.00), *Campbell Red Lake* ($30.25), *Homestake* ($58.13)—which

are probably overvalued on fundamentals but which would likely perform well if and because the South Africans acted poorly;

3. 5% the French Emprunt d'Etat 7% 1973 gold-backed bond;
4. 50% bullion, preferably in the form of low-premium bullion coins such as the Krugerrand, in view of their portability, divisibility, and typically the absence of the need for assaying. This position in effect represents a "hedge within the hedge."

In view of the vulnerability of the share prices to a decline in the bullion price, we continue to prefer long, and, to a lesser extent, intermediate life mines. (Please see data for all mines on page 135). I recognize that these mines represent low-leverage exposure if the gold price escalation is sustained or continues, and, on that basis, include a number of higher-risk, higher-leveraged short-life producers for those investors prepared to recognize and acept the greater risks involved. Thus, I would break down South African mine exposure as follows:

Group I (75% of total)—Long-life (20+ years) low-leverage, high yielders at lower gold price.

Group II (20% of total)—Medium-life (15-20 years) moderate yielders at lower gold price.

Group III (5% of total)—Speculative. High-leveraged short-life mines (approximately 6 years).

MKT. PRICE	MONTH	DOLLAR COST AVERAGE	UNIT COST AVERAGE
$200/oz.	1	1.000 oz./$200 = 200	1 @ $200 = $200
$300/oz.	2	.666 oz./$200 = 200	1 @ $300 = $300
$400/oz/	3	.500 oz./$200 = 200	1 @ $400 = $400
$600/oz.	4	.333 oz./$200 = 200	1 @ $600 = 600
$800/oz/	5	.250 oz./$200 = 200	1 @ $800 = $800
$700/oz.	6	.286 oz./$200 = 200	1 @ $700 = $700
$600/oz.	7	.333 oz./$200 = 200	1 @ $600 = $600
$500/oz.	8	.400 oz./$200 = 200	1 @ $50C = $500
$600/oz.	9	.333 oz./$200 = 200	1 @ $600 = $600
$700/oz.	10	.286 oz./$200 = 200	1 @ $700 = $700

| $540 | | 4.387   2000   2000 | 10 oz.   5400   5400 |

average cost of gold for 10 months—$540

average price per oz.—$455.89

average price per oz.—$540

* dollar cost averaging works best while systematically buying in an upward trending market that has normal up & down price fluctuations. Unit cost averaging out performs DCA when the price runs up with few price setbacks.

Silver was perhaps the first monetary metal, its use as such extending back almost six thousand years. This use probably began in the Middle East where it was used as a medium of exchange by merchants traveling by caravan who weighed out the metal itself. The standard measure of weight was the shekel, which is mentioned in the code of Hammurabi (Babylonian King, circa 2000 B.C.) and the term came into common usage as an Assyrian, Babylonian and Hebrew unit of weight and money.

A shekel amounted to about one-fiftieth of a mina. Later it became the name of a standard silver coin when coinage came into common use. Silver mining developed early in Asia Minor, and the technique then was brought to Spain by the Phoenicians who established colonies in Carthaginia (now Tunis and Morocco). In ancient times, extensive trade developed with India, whose spices, silver, cotton, ivory and jewels were much in demand. This resulted in a large quantity of silver finding its way into India where estimates (not very accurate) place the holdings at about four billion ounces. Most of this is in private hands and has been converted into jewelry and other ornaments.

With the conquest of Mexico and South America by the Spanish explorers in the 1500's, large amounts of silver were found in Mexico, Peru and Bolivia which were exploited and swelled the silver holdings of the world. Then great deposits were found in Nevada, in the United States, in the late 1800's which greatly expanded the world's silver supply.

These discoveries of silver in the southwestern United States led to much political controversy

Chapter XII

Silver As An Investment

Throughout man's history silver has been close-ly associated with gold, in terms of money and as a storage for value. Along with gold, it has been a sought-after monetary metal.

But today there is a different situation. Since the United States government stopped minting silver coins in the 1960's and, especially since it closed the silver window on January 24, 1968, when it ceased redeeming silver certificates for the metal itself, silver can no longer be regarded as a monetary metal.

There are four basic ways to invest in silver—bullion, coins, silver mining stocks and the futures market. We will consider each in turn.

and goverment intervention the story of which, while interesting, is not especially useful to detail here.

Suffice it to say that in 1934 the United States government nationalized silver, and ordered domestic holders, other than industrial users, to turn it in for fity cents an ounce. The New York Commodity Exchange dropped trading in silver. Such trading was not resumed until 1963 when all restrictions on silver ownership and trading were lifted.

As the commodity which it now is, silver fluctuates in price almost wholly dependent upon supply and demand factors.

Supply comes from the following sources:
1. Newly mined production.
2. Old scrap.
3. New scrap.
4. Existing stores of the metal.

Demand comes from the following quarters:
1. Photography.
2. Electrical and electronic manufacturing.
3. Household silverware and jewelry.
4. Brazing alloys.
5. Collectors' arts, coinage and medallions.

The source of newly mined silver is shown as follows:

Silver Mine Production by Country
(Million Troy Oz.)

	1973	1972	1971
Canada	48.0	47.0	45.9
Peru	40.0	39.0	38.4
U.S.S.R.	42.0	40.0	39.0
Mexico	38.5	37.5	36.7

U.S.	37.5	37.2	41.6
Australia	22.1	22.8	21.7
Japan	11.0	10.0	11.3
Other	68.3	66.6	64.1
Total	307.4	300.1	298.7

It is estimated that world production will increase in 1974 by about 7 million ounces to a total of 314 million ounces.

The most important thing to bear in mind about silver mining is that most new production results as a subsidiary aspect of the mining of copper, zinc, and lead. In other words, new supplies of silver do not result from demand for silver, but come about because of the demand for those other metals. Some small production does come from silver mines *per se* and also as a by-product of gold mining.

The increasing scarcity of workable silver ores and the high development costs for opening up new mines, or increasing the production of old ones, is likely to inhibit any great increase in the new production of silver.

Production of silver from old scrap is that which comes from used-up manufactured materials containing silver, such as contacts from old electrical apparatus, old photographic films, obsolete electric batteries, old household sterling ware and jewelry. Silver from new scrap comes from waste in new stampings, recovery from alloys, anode ends, plating solutions and the like.

Increasing demand and higher prices can bring about some expanded production from both old and new scrap sources by stimulating greater interest and efficiency in recovery processes on the part of industrial users. In fact, production of silver from processing scrap has been increasing over the past several years. According to reliable estimates, production from scrap in 1973 was about 10 million ounces, and in 1974 may reach 140 million ounces.

The amount of silver stores existing above ground is very large but almost impossible to ascertain accurately. This stock of silver exists chiefly in coins and as bullion. It is roughly estimated that 400 to 500 million ounces are held by Americans in the form of coins. Probably another 300 million ounces are privately held as coins in other countries. Under present circumstances experts think that, for a variety of reasons, there is little likelihood that this hoard will be a source of supply in the foreseeable future—unless the price of silver rises very dramatically.

The United States government holds about 180 million ounces of silver of which 139.5 million is in the strategic stockpile. There is pending much-debated legislation to reduce this stockpile. However, the opposition to this in Congress and other factors make the passage of such legislation unlikely. In any event, if some of the stockpile is put on the market it would not have much effect for any long period of time. Foreign holdings of silver are either not significantly large, nor are they believed likely to come on the market in sufficient amounts to have any long-term significant effects. This is believed to be true even of the large holdings in India.

The emerging pattern of demand for silver may be seen from the following percentage breakdown for the United States:

	1962	1972
Photography	31%	28%
Electrical Products	21%	26%
Sterling Ware	26%	16%
Brazing Alloys	11%	8%
Electroplated Ware	7%	8%
Miscellaneous	4%	14%

World silver consumption has been as follows:

Silver Consumption by Country
(Million Troy Oz.)

Industrial Uses

	1973	1972	1971
United States	190.0	151.1	129.1
Canada	8.5	7.4	6.0
Mexico	11.5	6.0	5.1
United Kingdom	31.5	27.5	25.0
France	22.5	20.0	15.6
West Germany	60.0	60.0	59.9
Italy	33.5	32.0	30.5
Japan	67.5	54.3	46.5
India	13.0	13.0	16.0
Other Countries	25.0	20.0	17.7
Total Industrial Uses	463.0	391.3	351.4

Coinage

	1973	1972	1971
United States	1.5	2.3	2.5
Canada	1.5	0.1	0.2
Austria	6.0	6.3	4.2
France	1.0	0.8	0.4
West Germany	6.0	24.0	17.9
Other Countries	3.5	3.0	2.0
Total Coinage Uses	20.0	36.5	27.2
Total Demand	483.0	427.8	378.6

In 1974 it is expected to be about 526 million ounces. United States silver consumption has been as follows:

U.S. Silver Consumption by End Use
(Million Troy Oz.)

	1973		1972		1971	
Photography	48.0	25.3%	38.3	25.4%	36.0	28%
Electrical & Electronic	47.0	24.7	42.5	28.1	33.5	26
Sterling Ware	28.0	14.7	22.1	14.6	20.0	15
Commemorative & Collector Arts	23.0	12.1	11.5	7.6	8.0	6
Electro Plated Ware	15.0	7.9	12.7	8.4	11.0	9
Brazing Alloys	14.0	7.4	12.2	8.1	12.0	9
Jewelry	6.0	3.2	4.9	3.2	3.5	3
Miscellaneous	9.0	4.7	6.9	4.6	5.0	4
	190.0	100.0	151.1	100.0	129.0	100

In 1974 it is expected to be 208.5 million ounces.

Consideration of the foregoing shows that for many years past there has been a growing gap between production of supplies of silver and demand for its use.

This deficit has been as follows:

      1971—42,000,000 ounces
      1972—77,000,000 ounces
      1973—120,000,000 ounces

The estimated deficit for 1974 is 140,000,000 ounces.

All of the foregoing indicates that there is a substantial trend in the demand for the use of silver to exceed available supplies—an equation which in market economics leads to higher prices. Couple these considerations with the ongoing inflation and it is evident why many predict much higher prices for silver in the not far distant future—as much as ten dollars per ounce by the end of this decade.

However, it is well to consider the contrary view summed up by a situation report of Merrill Lynch, Pierce, Fenner and Smith, Inc., dated March, 1974, which concludes:

"Long range price projections must place greater emphasis on basic fundamentals. In the past, these forecasts have often suggested higher prices. This reasoning was based mostly upon a characteristic of the basic supply/demand picture, namely chronic deficit production and the seemingly inescapable conclusion that silver supplies would eventually tighten. Using simple logic, market observers argued that as deficit outturn eroded stocks, prices would rise to levels that either curtailed demand or permitted the opening of high-cost mines. However, the booming silver prices scored in early 1974 have caused the premature realization of some popular long range price forecasts. This has resulted in a changed long term outlook. The unfolding view now suggests lower overall silver prices, based upon the following considerations:

"(1) The sharp price gains scored earlier this year have carried silver to levels whereby almost all of the 4.4 billion ounces of domestic silver reserves can be mined profitably. This will take a few years in many instances.

"(2) High prices coupled with the recent lifting of export restrictions will probably cause a sharp increase in the flow of silver from India. It has been estimated that India's silver holdings in jewelry and other forms top the three billion ounce level.

"(3) The likelihood that silver production in Mexico, Peru, Canada and elsewhere will also ultimately increase sharply because of prices.

"(4) The possibility of diminished buying because of reduced industrial consumption prompted by expected slower economic conditions and high prices.

"(5) The recent lifting of the oil embargo and the possibility of lower crude oil prices are two ingredients which suggests an improved economic climate. A key ingredient from silver's viewpoint is the rate of inflation and the ability of government to check rising prices. Evidence that inflation rates are subsiding would remove the major force behind silver purchases, namely speculative buying encouraged by the erosion of purchasing power of currencies.

"(6) The possibility that Congress will authorize the sale of 117 million ounces of silver from the U.S. stockpile in the not too distant future."

However, there are many others who are convinced that the deficit in silver production will increase and that the negative factors quoted above will not come into play in sufficient strength to reduce such deficits substantially. Indeed, they believe that the shortage will be so great that many companies will find themselves in a disastrous situation. They point out that the inventory of silver held by the New York Commodity Exchange dropped in 1973 from 125,000,000 ounces to 50,000,000 ounces. Also, that as prices go up, hoarders become even more reluctant to sell.

From the foregoing it may be seen that investing in silver involves different considerations from those involved in investing in gold. Since silver is now basically a commodity—albeit a relatively scarce and valuable one—it is not the straightforward hedge against inflation that gold is.

Before plunging into silver one must study the factors and weigh the risks—the rewards could be great.

There are problems facing the buyer of silver bullion of which he should be aware. In the first place you can store it yourself or have the seller store it for you. In any event, being bulky this presents some problems. Bullion is commonly purchased in the form of ingots weighing 1,000 ounces (about 55 pounds), at spot prices plus $100 to $350 per bar. A bar of bullion might be difficult to sell because of questions of authenticity. In the Chicago futures market you must buy in 5,000 ounce lots at the cost of a commission of $35.50. In New York the minimum quantity dealt in is 10,000 ounces with a commission cost of $45.50. Dealers' commissions will vary, but are generally around 2%. Storage charges and insurance can work out to considerable sums over any lengthy period of time.

Investing in Silver Coins

Silver coins have become a favorite investment medium in recent years. They present some advantages over bullion for the average investor willing to speculate on an advance in the price of silver and as an inflation hedge.

The chief advantages are that:

1. The coins can never drop below their face value as money even if silver declines steeply in price.

2. Coins are readily indentifiable and the question of their authenticity cannot arise.

3. If there should be hyperinflation then they can be spent in small amounts.

For these reasons silver coins are likely to sell much of the time at a premium over their silver content value.

Some facts:

° U.S. silver dimes, quarters, half-dollars, and dollars minted in 1964 or before are 90% silver.

° It is legally permissible to melt them down— this costs a few pennies per ounce.

° Silver dollars, and to a lesser extent half-dollars, have some collectors' value and there are fewer of them than dimes and quarters, so they usually sell at some premium over the smaller coins. So dimes and quarters are usually the better buys.

° Sales are in bags of $1,000 face value of coins, smaller than a volleyball and weighing about 55 pounds.

° The silver refined content is about 720 ounces.

° As the price of silver rises, the premium above the silver content tends to diminish; and paradoxically, for technical market reasons, there have been times when silver, in coin form, has sold for a little under that in bullion form. But this is an anomaly that never can last for a long period

° Commission on purchases of bags of silver coins from dealers is usually about 2%, but it is necessary to be aware of hidden charges and also to make sure that the price charged is the legitimate spot price.

° The largest market in silver coins is made by the New York Mercantile Exchange (on which are traded many other commodities in large volume). However on this highly legitimate exchange, coins must be bought or sold in ten-bag lots. The commission is $3.50 per bag. Taking delivery is complicated but can be arranged.

° There are a number of silver coin dealers who advertise extensively having the word "exchange" in their name but they are not exchanges in the same general, regulated sense as the New York Mercantile Exchange, even though they do permit a customer to buy on margin—typically 25% or less. When bought on margin from these dealers the customer must pay interest on the unpaid balance and storage charges in addition—even though the dealer may not be actually storing anything but has covered his liability to the customer by purchasing coins for future delivery on the commodities exchanges.

° A big disadvantage in operating with a dealer is that you may not be able to sell your bags of coins to any dealer other than the one from whom you bought.

The dealer's price is made by him and while related to the commodities exchange equivalent price, such price is likely to be different on any particular day.

The New York Times, on July 11, 1974, reported that the New York State Attorney General was investigating the possibility of large-scale fraudulent practices by silver coin dealers. The article quotes Nicholas L. Deak, head of the Deak-Perera Group of companies, which operate in all aspects of the money market as follows:

"Many turned to silver coins and this tempted the brokers and dealers to take more orders than they filled, covering themselves by some such devices as trading in the silver futures market, or not covering themselves. Silver bars and silver coins do tend to move up and down in price together—but there are times when they don't. For there is current production in silver bars, whereas there is only past production in silver coins. Silver trading is a very risky business."

Bearing in mind all the foregoing, it may well be that you will want to own a few bags of silver coins anyway. If you do decide to purchase them be careful to calculate carefully and heed the warnings.

Investments in Silver Mining Stocks
There is no publicly-held widely traded company of significant size that is engaged only in silver mining. But there are a few natural resource companies for whom silver is a major product.

These represent an opportunity for investment for those who expect the price of silver to rise and wish to benefit therefrom. Some of the better grade companies in this category are:

Hecla Mining Co.

Traded on the New York Stock Exchange, this company is the most important silver producer in the United States. Its chief operation is the production of silver and lead, but it also produces gold, zinc, and other metals and has a substantial interest in Canadian and Arizona copper mines. It also has good uranium prospects.

Hecla earned $.44 per share in the first quarter of 1974—almost equal to its earnings for the entire second half of 1973. If the price of silver averages $4.50 per ounce for the year 1974 Hecla could earn from $1.60 to $1.80 for the year. It is making heavy capital investments in new ventures which will probably keep its dividends limited to the 2% in stock which it pays currently.

Sunshine Mining Company

Traded on the New York Stock Exchange, this company operates the largest silver mine in the United States, which it owns together with Hecla and another company. It is also engaged in a number of other businesses unrelated to silver mining. Some analysts think that participation in this company's prospects are bright through its convertible debentures—the 6½s of '89. First quarter 1974 earnings were $1,100,000, four times interest requirements. The bonds are convertible at 54.3 shares of common for each $1,000 bond.

The bonds could benefit from a rise in the price of silver and also any future turning down of interest rates.

Fresnillo

Traded on the American Stock Exchange, this company produces silver, lead, and zinc. Its silver mine is probably short-life but it has interests in a group of Mexican mines thought to have substantial silver and gold ores.

This company earned $2.50 per share in 1973 and $1.04 in the first quarter of 1974 (excluding some non-recurring additional profits). It may earn $3.50 to $4.00 per share in 1974, and pays a dividend of $.20 a share quarterly plus 5% in stock.

United Keno Hill Mines

Traded over-the-counter and on the Toronto Stock Exchange this company produced 3.1 million ounces of silver in 1973, making it a major Canadian Silver mine. Its total revenues of over $10 million was more than double that of 1972. It showed a net profit of $1.11 per share in 1973 payijg a dividend of $.40 which was a dramatic turn around from its loss of $.29 per share in 1972.

For the six months ending June 30, 1974, the company reported net profits of $1.66 per share compared to $.39 per share for the first six months of 1973.

This company is 48% owned by Falconbridge and is well financed.

Rosario Resources

This company earned $1.53 per share in 1973 compared to $.59 per share in 1972—an increase of 159%.

It produces gold, silver, lead, zinc and cadmium from mines in Mexico, Honduras, The Dominican Republic and Nicaragua. Through subsidiaries it has oil and gas reserves and concessions in Canada, United States, Africa and the North Sea.

A new processing plant, in which it has invested $24 million, to be completed this year will be able to handle the production of 350,000 ounces of gold and 150,000 ounces of silver.

For the six months ending June 30, 1974, earnings were $1.21 compared to $.59 for the first six months of 1973. This company has paid dividends every year since 1896. The current dividend is $.40 per share.

American Smelting and Refining Co.

This is a high-quality natural resource company traded on the New York Stock Exchange (popularly known as ASARCO). It is the world's largest smelter of non-ferrous metals.

It is often overlooked that this huge mining complex has very large interests in silver, having produced 7,936,000 ounces in 1972, including 4,222,000 from the Galena Mine, the second largest silver mine in the United States. In addition, through affiliated companies, including a 49% interest in Asarco-Mexicana, which produced 15.5 million ounces in 1972, and further production is expected through the development of a mine in Ontario, Canada in a 60-40 partnership with Anaconda Company. Asarco is also a large refiner of silver.

Investment in this company provides a high quality opportunity to participate, at least partially, in any expected silver boom.

Trading Silver Futures

Commodity trading—including silver and silver coins—is a form of speculation attractive to many. It is a very technical, specialized occupation which should not be engaged in, except with great care after thorough study. Both the risks and the rewards are very great—and both are exaggerated because trading can be done on very low margins. This is not a game for amateurs. For a glimpse at such trading here is how one day's activity looks, as reported in *The Wall Street Journal* of August 2, 1974:

	Open	High	Low	Close	Change	Season's High	Low

NEW YORK—SILVER

	Open	High	Low	Close	Change	Season's High	Low
Aug.	500.00	504.00	468.00	470.50	—24.80	621.00	390.00
Sept.	503.50	504.00	480.20	480.20	—20.00	649.40	231.00
Dec.	518.00	519.00	495.00	495.00	—20.00	652.10	274.80
Jan. 75	522.50	522.50	498.00	498.80	—20.00	653.00	276.90
Mar.	531.00	531.00	506.50	506.50	—20.00	655.20	291.50
May	537.00	537.50	513.30	513.30	—20.00	657.00	342.80
July	542.50	542.50	519.40	519.40	—20.00	659.40	423.00
Sept.	549.00	549.00	525.50	525.50	—20.00	650.00	433.50
Dec.	560.00	560.00	534.30	534.30	—20.00	560.00	534.30

Sales: 4,588 contracts.

SILVER COIN FUTURES (IN DOLLARS)

	Open	High	Low	Close	Change	Season's High	Low
Oct.	3590	3604	3405	3405	—150	4570	1731
Jan. 75	3710	3713	3520	3521	—149	4630	2145
Apr.	3826	3826	3625	3625	—150	4685	2200
July	3740	3740	3732	3720a	—145	4730	3100
Oct.	3990	3990	3990	3805a	—145	4300	3155

Sales: 142 contracts.

Informative literature regarding commodity trading generally, and in silver and coins in particular, is available on request from larger reputable brokers such as Merrill Lynch, Pierce, Fenner and Smith, Inc.

Here are some responsible views concerning the prospects for silver:

Merrill Lynch, Pierce, Fenner, and Smith, Inc., in a report published in March 1974, concludes:

"However, the booming silver prices scored in early 1974 have caused the premature realization of some popular long-range price forecasts. This has resulted in a changed long-term outlook. The unfolding view now suggests lower over-all silver prices . . ."

Hayden Stone Inc., in its extensive 1974 study believes:

"The supply/demand balance for silver is very constructive and should continue that way . . . Over the long term, both supply/demand data and monetary and emotional factors suggest a continuing scenario for higher prices, reaching possibly $8-10 an ounce over the next several years."

The Holt Investment Advisory (July 9, 1974) sees silver rising again to $6 an ounce, and higher, over the next 6 to 12 months and recommends to cool-headed investors, Fresnillo, Hecla, and Sunshine.

Chapter XIII

A Survey of Experts' Opinions of Gold as an Investment

Here are presented the views of a great variety of analysts respecting the desirability of investing in gold at the present time. Necessarily these are excerpts. It is suggested that anyone desiring to learn the reasons behind these views can obtain them by proper inquiry.

Merrill Lynch, Pierce, Fenner & Smith Inc.

In a report entitled "Gold Review," dated May 2, 1974, signed David J. Fitzpatrick, European Securities Research:

"CONCLUSION: We believe that higher free-market prices for gold will ultimately lead to higher official prices for transactions between the central banks of Europe and of the Western World in general. Our long-term bullishness rests primarily on supply-demand considerations for the metal, however. The prospect of a higher official gold price is really an added bonus."

This report was followed by a research report dated June 13, 1974, signed by David Fitzpatrick and James Waterman, which was published after the June meeting of the International Monetary Fund's Committee of Ten finance ministers of the major trading nations. On June 11, 1974, it was agreed that gold may be used as collateral for international borrowing at a price set by the lending nation, which necessarily would be at free-market prices. Other agreements were also arrived at that meeting. The report concludes:

"CONCLUSIONS—These recent developments can be regarded as encouraging. Near-term gold prices may, in fact, go lower and test the $150 level particularly since as much as 800 tons have been accumulated by speculators and investors in the last 18 months. The longer term outlook remains encouraging, however, in our opinion. Treasury Secretary Simon has suggested that U.S. citizens be allowed to own bullion. Although it would be wrong to regard such a development as assured, the implication can only be regarded as bullish given the size of United States buying power relative to new gold supplies on the free market." *Drexel, Burnham & Co., Incorporated.*

In a report of 35 closely-packed pages entitled "Gold-Related Investments" dated February, 1980, signed by Andre Sharon (republished in condensed form in this reprinting of Gold For The Millions, it is concluded:

"*POINT OF VIEW*—South African gold shares may represent a worthwhile 'hedge' against both inflation, and eventually, deflation. Many of them also possess a number of *positive* attributes including, (if the gold price remains firm), frequently attractive dividend yields. Given ever-present but unquantifiable political risks, and relatively thin capitalizations, and because we remain optimistic about the capacity of our system to overcome its difficulties, we flatly reject the position of those who place the bulk of their assets in gold and related issues. We suggest placing only a limited portion of portfolios in a selected 'package' of South African gold mining stocks, the percentage being a function of an individual's own assessment of the situation, including its irrational aspects."

Shearson, Loeb Rhoades, Inc.

In a report as of March, 1974, entitled "Silver-Gold, How High is Up?" it is stated under the heading, "Conclusions":

"Gold's supply/demand balance is also quite constructive. Primary mine production has been declining recently. The addition of new facilities in South Africa and Canada in 1974 should be of some help but the lack of new rich ore sources coupled with a reluctance to open new facilities due to high costs and uncertainties should keep the primary production outlook far from bright. Secondary production is a relatively small source of gold but will undoubtedly continue to grow rapidly. World gold stocks are very large but are unlikely to provide much gold for industrial use. Privately held stocks can even be a source of demand especially in light of increased Arab revenues from the hike in crude oil prices. Government supplies could provide some relief, but at this point, the only commodity that is coming out of the central bankers is talk. This trend is likely to continue. The outlook is for more growth in industrial demand with jewelry and electrical uses leading the way. The monetary and emotional sources of demand are likely to escalate, especially if and when U.S. citizens are permitted to own gold.

"The price of gold may decline near term, on the basis of a somewhat cooled world situation, a slowing of the inflationary fires and an economic slowdown in the industrial world. For the longer term, however, given a constructive supply/demand balance, strong monetary and emotional demand and the effects of probable legalized U.S. gold ownership, prospects are for higher (possibly very much higher) prices over the next few years."

American Institute Counselors Inc.
(Great Barrington, Mass. 01230)

In its quarterly "Review of Investment Policy, dated April 15, 1974 this publication advises:

> "Gold stocks: The risks involved in other investments have become so great that we consider some gold stocks advisable for all investors. We believe that shares of selected foreign gold mining companies and investment trusts that invest most of their funds in such shares provide the best obtainable protection for a portion of one's funds against future depreciation in buying power of the dollar and/or the possibility of a severe recession or depression. A copy of our Gold Portolio presenting analyses of gold stocks is available at $10."

The Holt Investment Advisory
(Published by T.J. Holt & Company,
277 Park Avenue, New York, New York, 10017)

In its February 1, 1974 issue, this publication, as a special feature, reprinted a speech of Mr. Holt given at a symposium sponsored by The National Committee to Legalize Gold, held in New Orleans on January 19, 1974. The speech is a long one, and covered broad aspects of the economic scene. In the course of this talk, Mr. Holt remarks:

> "Now, don't get me wrong, ladies and gentlemen. *And please don't quote me out of context.* I am, and always have been, a strong advocate of gold as a standard and a store of value. I have always been a vocal champion

of sound money. And I have consistently told my clients to invest heavily in precious metal stocks ever since the pound sterling was first devalued in late 1967. In 1968 and 1969, when 'gold' was a dirty word on Wall Street, our firm ran a promotional campaign in some 20 newspapers and magazines across the country with the headline 'GOLD PRICES MUST SOAR.'

"Furthermore, I'm quite convinced that the prices of gold and gold stocks will yet be pushed up spectacularly by the gold rush of this generation. Sometime this spring, or summer, I believe, there'll be a gold-buying panic. Whether the price will be driven to $200 or $300 or $400 an ounce, frankly, I don't know. But it will certainly be far, far above today's quotation. Gold stocks and coins, of course, will also skyrocket.

"But it is precisely because I anticipate this blow-off occurring later this year, that I now foresee the distinct possibility—indeed the high probability—of gold stocks coming down when deflation finally takes hold."

In the June 19, 1974 issue of his advisory letter, Mr. Holt follows up his ideas on the subject of gold as follows:

"All in all, then, we look for a major upsurge in the price of gold to unfold this summer— an upsurge that will dwarf last winter's mini-fever. The retreat of the gold price in recent months has been a perfectly normal correction process, shaking out the weak holders.

"Significantly, even with gold prices stabilizing, at, say, $150 an ounce, most South African producers can count on luscious profits for years. And unlike many other industrial companies, such profits are likely to hold, even after a world-wide depression is on the way. Meanwhile we believe the eventual permanent price will probably be in the neighborhood of $175.00 an ounce."

The International Harry Schultz Letter
(Published by Financial and Economic
    Research Corporation, P.O. Box 1161,
    Basel, 4002, Switzerland)
This publication was one of the first to sing the values of gold to beat inflation and each issue of Mr. Schultz's letter continues to vociferously recommend gold and make specific recommendations concerning how to invest in it. In his issue #327, early November, 1974, his asset distribution recommendation was as follows:

Bank Deposits   30%
    Demand deposits—5%
    Eurocurrency time deposits—25%

Equities (trading)   10%
    Campbell Red Lake, Homestake

Equities (golds)   45%
  Quality South African Golds:
  Doornfontein, President Steyn,
  Winkelhaak, Harmony,
  Randfontein, Amgold

  Mining Finance:
  Gold Fields of South Africa

  Canadian Golds:
  Goldex, Agnico-Eagle, Dome

  High Yield Golds:
  Bracken, Kinross, Western Holdings

  High Leveraged Golds:
  East Rand Proprietary, South Africa
  Land, Durban Deep, Venterspost, Leslie,
  South Vaal, Marievale, Wits Nigel

Miscellaneous   15%
  Gold coins/gold bullion (Austrian Krong,
  Mexican Peso, Krugerrand)
Lynch International Investment Survey
(120 Broadway, New York, New York 10005)
  In its issue of January 28, 1974 this service advised:

"Certainly in this period of continuing economic and monetary uncertainty, investors should maintain their gold positions, despite the very sharp increases that have occurred in the past two months. We expect price reactions from these very high levels. However gold share investments over the long term will continue to be sound."

United Business Service
(210 Newbury Street, Boston, Mass. 02116)

In a "Special Release" in April 1974, this service said the following:

"The rise in gold has been the most exciting, perhaps because it was so long forecast. For more than a generation after the price was frozen by governmental action at $35 per ounce, 'gold bugs' have predicted that, once released from such artificial control, gold would soar to as much as $70 or even $100 per ounce. When the metal was released it went from $34.75 to $124 in just 48 months, far outdoing the expectation of its most ardent admirers."

". . . GOLD. Inflation and loss of confidence in world paper currency are the key to this market, and what ultimately happens depends on how the former is contained and the latter fortified. The recent rise from $90 to $178 was extremely fast and shows the explosive ability of gold. But because it was so fast, an erratic phase—characterized by sizable price changes up and down—could easily develop. However, with the monetary situation still precarious, and fears of hyperinflation prevalent the longer outlook is bullish."

At the end of 1973, the Wall Street Transcript, 120 Wall Street, New York, New York 10005, held a roundtable discussion on gold in which the participants were C. Austin Barker of Hornblower and Weeks-Hemphill, Noyes, Incorporated, John C. Van Eck of International Investors Inc., Dr. Franz Pick, publisher of *Pick's Currency Yearbook* and *Pick's Currency Report*, Otto E. Roethenmund of Deak & Co. Inc., Deson Sze, of Harris, Upham & Co. Incorporated, and William H. Tehan of P.R. Herzig and Company.

Again, in June, 1974, the Wall Street Transcript conducted another roundtable on the subject of gold, in which the participants were: Nicholas Deak, of Deak & Perera Corporations, Donald B. McShane, president of McShane & Co., A. James Meigs, vice-president and economist at Argus Research Corporation, James E. Sinclair, a general partner of Vilas & Hickey, and William H. Tehan, gold mining and monetary analyst at P.R. Herzig & Co. Transcripts of both of these roundtable discussions are available at a small cost from the Wall Street Transcript. Both discussions are very enlightening; however quotations will be taken only from the later roundtable.

Some quotations from Mr. Tehan's remarks:

". . . My point is that the domestic problems facing the United States Government, from a political point of view of rising unemployment and deflation, will be so acute that the Fed will expand credit on a massive scale. Franklin Roosevelt said in the 1930's that he didn't care about the fetishes of international bankers. Arthur Burns, or whoever succeeds him, will have the same attitude. So the expansion of credit in the United States banking system to hopefully finance a domestic recovery from depression will be so massive that it will create a situation whereby you just can't restructure a monetary system."

". . . I agree with Nick that the price is going to rise, but I think it's going to rise under the force of a credit crisis and collapse. In other words, a money panic in which currencies and bank deposits will be converted into bullion, in anticipation of bank closures, the practical experience of bankruptcies, defaults on bonds, etc. I'm looking for a very serious deflation ahead, but a rise in gold is a consequence of a credit liquidation."

". . . it's hard to say. I would say that probably next year we will see gold at around $300 an ounce; $280 to $300 would be my guess."

"Trending up. I wouldn't argue with Nick; in four or five years you would see it around $500. I just use those figures as an indication of the magnitude of the rise. If you recall in our first meeting I said in a few years we would see gold around $150. I couldn't exactly pinpoint it."

". . . The United States Treasury, in August 1971, said we will no longer take dollars back in exchange for gold, which we had pledged to do. In September the Japanese floated the yen. They said we would no longer give dollar quotes. What these central banks were all saying was we don't want to take any more currency. If they sell gold now, they will be taking currency. There is no reason for them to reverse the policy that was expressed in the market action of floating in 1971. What they want is an asset that may appreciate, that is liquid and stable, and I contend that no central bank will sell bullion."

". . . I would buy coins that offer you a good bullion value, like the Austrian 100 Krone, the Austrian Four Ducat, the One Ducat Krone, the Mexican peso and the British sovereign, which has a high premium, but it's still a good investment.

"I would not buy high-premium munismatic coins, because in a deflation those premiums will come down, though not advance when the price of gold is rising, or an actual decline.

"In terms of gold mining shares I would certainly buy the good quality shares, President Steyn, President Brand, Vaal Reefs, St. Helena. And for certain accounts, some of the more leveraged mines. Whether you buy them depends on the nature of the account, East Rand Proprietary, Grootvlei, Venterspost.

"I don't go too heavily into Canadian. I think Camflo is an excellent quality Canadian mine, and Pamour is very good. By and large, I concentrate my gold mining investments in South Africa."

Nicholas Deak:
"I agree with most of the economists I have spoken to, that the price of gold, before this year is over, will be over $200. And it will creep up and go up in the same proportion as our government will continue to pump more money in circulation. And the velocity of the circulation of the money will depend again, as it has been pointed out here, on the lack of faith in the money. Because money is spent faster and faster, as the faith in the money decreases. And in the next three years the price of gold will go well over $400 and $500. The rate of inflation will increase.

"As far as gold coins are concerned there are two schools of thought: Those who have no specific knowledge of gold coins, which have been mentioned before, either 50 peso Mexican, the 100 Kronen Austrian. The Austrian ducats are not as good, but they are fairly good still. The new gold coins which are coming out now, and have exactly the same gold content as the Austrians, are the Hungarian hundred crown. They started restriking them, minting them, just a few weeks ago, and they are already here in the United States. And of course the sovereigns, but the sovereigns have a little bit higher premium. And those who are knowledgeable in gold coins will buy gold coins with high numismatic value, and they probably will find as much satisfaction or more satisfaction than those who concentrate on bullion-type coins. When and if ownership of gold is permitted in the United States, I think there will be an influx of small gold bars. And when the price surges up, there will be a shortage of all these things temporarily."

Donald B. McShane:

"In other words, I'm talking about a segmented collapse in the economy. I think you are going to see a crisis in the banking system. I think you are seeing it now. I think you are seeing it as part of the deflation right now in certain segments of the market. Inventories are high now which tend to over-dramatize temporary shortages. But the economy is even less able to accept the restrictive policies of the Fed today than in 1970-1971, so they will have to ease shortly. In my scenario, I see gold in 12 months between $250 and $300 an ounce, on its way toward $500 an ounce maybe two or three years down the road.

James Sinclair:

"I see a floor in gold coming in at certain levels for psychological reasons. That floor, in my opinion, will be the market-related price at which gold is exchanged between central banks of the European economic community, in settlement of external obligations. That's been indicated to us by Witveen of the I.M.F., promised to us by Larre of the Bank of International Settlement, promised to us by Haferkamp of the E.E.C. When these men promise such possibilities, you can gather it's a probability.

"I think inflation will be running in double digit form, between 10 and 18 per cent—considered to be very good when it comes down from 18 and considered difficult when it comes up from 10—vacillating between those two points. I think the absolute low you will see on gold this year, if this reaction continues, is $138 to $142. I would suggest that the high on this move will be $215 to $218, with a possible high this year between $236 and $242."

Joseph Granville

"But there is still one big question that bothers me. I suspect that many other governments of the world are waiting for the United States to set a new official price, which, in effect, would be to step in again, for the world to peg the price of gold in terms of goods and services. When we raised the price in the '30s the United States government put the price above the world free market price. We bought gold for a long time in order to hold the price up. Later it turned out that our price was lower than the free market price, and we sold gold for a long time, until we closed the window. And I just have the feeling that many of the central bankers and governments are hoping that we will put a new floor under the price, so then they can sell some gold without being afraid of being blamed for driving down the price."

In an article entitled, "In Case of Doubt, Buy Insurance" in *Forbes*, July 15, 1973, Walter Oechsle, vice-president of Arnhold, Bleichroeder, Inc., investment bankers, writes:

"I am unlikely to ever advise an all-out stance in favor of gold and gold shares. In my April 1972 column, I recommended gold shares as reasonable insurance against many other things going wrong. Today, with so much having gone wrong, the key questions are: Can the prevailing fears get any worse? Does the bear market in Wall Street have much further to go? If the answers are yes, then South African gold shares still do make sense. They have, in fact, been a very good hedge against bear markets in the past and are very likely to be countercyclical in the future. In other words, if you still consider the risk in U.S. equities to be substantial, gold shares are likely to be a better hedge than cash."

". . . I do not advise either aggressive or extensive accumulation of gold shares. Five percent to 10% of a given portfolio should probably be a maximum. Even that limited an exposure should make you sleep better if the bear market were to continue. Finally, don't forget that the best insurance is the one you do not need, and I hope that any insurance you take out now against further deterioration of the United States market will prove to be superfluous."

How interesting it is to read those words just one year later and to see how important the insurance referred to was! It now must look too bad that he advised only 5 or 10% in gold shares.

AND NOW FOR A CONTRARY OPINION, look at the *Argus Weekly Staff Report*, dated June 24, 1974, published by Argus Research Corporation, 140 Broadway, New York, New York 10005. Argus is one of the most influential and respected financial research organizations in the world. Its reports are directed chiefly to bankers and brokers, and it may be called an analyst's advisor.

The referred to report of Argus states as its opinion:

"There are, indeed, few ready buyers for large amounts of gold. The Arab states—particularly Saudi Arabia—have shown a highly modern approach to the question of what to do with their new riches. The Saudis have shown a clear intention to use it both for development and to integrate themselves into the Western economies. Thus, Kissinger's accommodative approach to the Arabs holds great promise for the stability of the international monetary system and bodes ill for gold. For, like other governments bent on development, the Arab states will find little use for the metal.

"Similarly, news that Americans—there are now 211 million of them—who have been barred from holding gold since 1933 may soon be permitted to return to the market should have increased the gold price. But it didn't. There are three reasons for this:

"° According to many experts, a substantial part of the U.S. public demand for gold is being met by gold coins and various other numismatic and commemorative objects.

"° When actually faced with the choice of holding gold, Americans, who have options to hold a wider variety of investments than citizens of other countries, will weigh the options rather carefully. They could easily conclude that the expected rate of return is too low.

"° Finally, Secretary of the Treasury William Simon has indicated that increased U.S. demand for gold could be met with increased supply out of the Treasury's own holdings. This would, of course, tend to increase the risk of holding gold.

"This is so even though the basic cause of gold fever—rapid depreciation of conventional monies around the world—continues at work. It is our opinion, however, that world inflation will decelerate toward the end of the year. And this could easily lead—when it occurs, or can clearly be anticipated—to further erosion in the value of this ancient metal.

"In our opinion, the world's problem is likely to continue to be inflation rather than deflation. We have for some months been predicting a decline in the inflation rate toward the end of the year. The implication of recent world economic events is to increase our confidence in this forecast."

Chapter XIV

What Does the Future Hold?

.

The question of buying gold or investing in gold mine stocks must be related to what you think the future course of the United States' and the World's economy is likely to be.

Up to now, the rule: "Don't Sell America Short" has worked very well despite severe temporary setbacks. Because of this, the American mind has been closed to the idea of accumulating gold or even thinking of gold in terms of an investment. This was in sharp contradistinction to the rest of the world which did not have the experience of developing a vast rich territory where a simple equation: Work + Investment = Prosperity—gave unlimited hope and the possiblity of realization of ambition to countless citizens. Gold was a static store of wealth—a medium for miserly hoarding or for expediting the esoteric workings of the financial machinery of international trade. After all, the price of gold had been fixed in 1717 by Sir Isaac Newton, who was Great Britain's Supervisor of the Mint, at $20 per ounce, and that continued to be the price util Great Britain went off the gold standard 200 years later in 1931. In 1933, President Roosevelt withdrew the right of Americans to own gold and in 1934 raised its centuries-old price to $35 per ounce.

None of this seriously affected the man in the street. Subsequent events vindicated the indifference to gold and the adage, "Don't sell America short." Yet all the while gold continued to play its role in the monetary system, until the drain on U.S. treasury stocks of the metal in 1970 and 1971 led to the closing of the gold window by President Nixon on August 15, 1971. This left the international monetary system bereft of the stabilizing and disciplinary role of gold. Since then the fires of inflation have been engulfing the world.

We now face an entirely new situation—no gold standard to restrain the printing presses, shortages of oil and food, unwritten but real commitments by all the Western countries to prevent high unemployment rates, etc.

Under these circumstances it is difficult not to be pessimistic concerning the future of the economy of the United States and the Western World.

What are the possibilities? Broadly speaking, they are three in number:

1. Amicable cooperation between these countries (including the oil producers) under the auspices of the International Monetary Fund. The new gold-free SDRs are accepted and serve their

intended function in replacing gold. Domestic "fine tuning" by each government, using fiscal and monetary policy, keeps each nation's inflation rate at reasonable levels. All of this leads to a new era of peace and prosperity.

Would you bet on it?

2. Gold is remonetized at a sufficiently high price to serve its function as money of last resort. To accomplish this, the price now would have to be more than $150 per ounce, and with each passing day witnessing ever increasing inflation that price would necessarily be much higher—$250, $300, $400 or more, as time goes on.

3. The spiraling collapse of all currencies, bringing about a world-wide depression of untold magnitude.

Even if you (wishfully) think that the first possibility can be accomplished, the other two alternatives cannot be ruled out and some investments should be made in gold and gold stocks if only as an insurance policy.

If you expect the second possibility (and if there is any intelligent direction of affairs by our leaders, then this will be the outcome) gold will hold its price and gold stocks will skyrocket as the mines will be assured of high-level profits and extended life, with such a floor under them.

If the last unthinkable alternative is to occur, then the only refuge is gold—and we had better hope that it will serve as the salvation it has been in past disasters.

It is true that investment in gold requires a pessimistic attitude—it gives no immediate return as do other conventional investments, such as bank deposits, stocks and bonds. How valid is it, to take a pessimistic attitude?

In *The New York Times*, June 23, 1974 Edwin L. Dale, Jr., in an article entitled "Q. & A. on the Prospects for a World Depression," writes:

"Washington—For the first time in a generation, some serious people are talking about the danger of a world slump or depression. *The Economist* of London, for example, describes the Labor Government of Harold Wilson as 'facing a deteriorating economic situation even grimmer than faced the last minority Labor Government in 1929-31—as big a slump, but with very serious inflation . . .

"Views such as these are distinctly in a minority, at least up to now. The 'standard' economic forecast in the United States, in and out of government, is for rising, not falling, output for the rest of 1974 and in 1975, though there are differences over how vigorous the economy will be. Still, everyone agrees that there are highly unusual features of the present situation, some of which may be dangerous . . .

"Q. What are the main causes of the global inflation? Does it affect the poor countries differently from the rich?

"A. The most important single cause of the global inflation is that all of the main coun-

tries, including the United States, pursued e
cessively expansionary fiscal and monetary
policies from about 1970 until 1973. Part of
this, outside of the United States, was inad-
vertent, a result of the death throes of the international monetary system based on fixed
currency exchange rates. Defending the old
rates had the indirect effect of greatly swell-
ing the money supply in countries such as
West Germany and Switzerland.

"In the end, global demand boomed so
strongly that prices of all kinds began to be
pulled upward, particularly the prices of numerous raw materials: copper, lead, tin, natural rubber, wool, cotton and the like. Many of
these prices at the wholesale level have begun
to turn down in the past few weeks, but final
retail prices still do not reflect the earlier
huge increases. For the consumer, then,
many prices are still certain to rise.

"In addition to the fundamental cause, two
special factors made the problem much worse
in 1973 and early 1974. Poor 1972 harvests in
several parts of the world cut the supply of
food at a time of booming global demand,
with the result of a steep rise in food prices,
which has now begun to abate.

"And, of course, in late 1973 the oil cartel
began to function, with devastating effects on
the price of oil and its products.

"Finally, in some countries such as Britain and Japan, though not until very recently in the United States, union-won wage increases far in excess of gains in productivity were an independent factor in inflation.

"Inflation has caused serious problems for all countries but it has been particularly severe on those poor nations that have not benefited from higher prices for the raw materials they export and that have to import food, fertilizer and fuel. For them, the problem is not only higher prices for their already-poor consumers, but finding enough foreign exchange to maintain a minimum volume of imports . . .

"Q. If there is a worsening of the general world economic situation, what will be the effect on the ordinary American?

"A. It depends on which way the situation worsens. If there is a global slump, including in the United States, the impact will fall on those who lose their jobs, while others would probably benefit in a sense, through a decline in inflation. If inflation continues or worsens, there will be a deterioration in the standard of living for all those, including many of the poor, whose incomes do not rise as fast as prices.

"While the American economy is closely connected with that of the rest of the world, it would still be possible for the United States to insulate itself at least to some extent from grave developments abroad. But it is also true that if the United States succeeds in moderating inflation without a serious slump, the chances for the rest of the world doing so are much brighter."

In an article in *The New York Times*, June 20, 1974, entitled, "The Sky is Falling," John M. Lee writes:

"Well, what is one to think of it all? Certainly, there is reason enough to mope. The seeds of inflation planted since, say, 1968, by the United States deficit in international payments, the system of fixed exchange rates and a worldwide lack of fiscal and monetary restraint, have produced the worst international inflation in history. The situation has been helped along by acts of God and Allah: The business cycles of major industrial nations, which swung up together to produce the extraordinary boom of 1972-73, have now swung down together.

"Business dislocations are inevitable, and these are occurring—in the housing industry, automobiles, utilities and the stock and bond markets. The question is whether these can be contained or do deeper troubles lie ahead?

"Anyone with a sense of historic parallel could look at last week's collapse of a big

West German private bank, Herstatt, and recall how the fall of the Harty financial group in London in early October, 1929, contributed to Wall Street's disintegration. Those on the lookout for the rock that starts the avalanche could ponder the near-default of the city of Rome on its massive debt."

An editorial entitled "Thinking About Depression" in *The Wall Street Journal*, July 22, 1974, discusses the same subject:

"Herman Kahn, the physicist and thinker who runs the Hudson Institute, believes there is one chance in six of a depression in 1974-75, and if it doesn't occur in this period, one chance in six that it will occur in 1976-1980. In other words, he sees one chance in three that in this decade we will experience depression, by which he means a 10% unemployment rate lasting at least 18 months. There are those who believe Mr. Kahn is being a pessimist; there also are some we talk to who think the chances are higher.

"Those who dismiss such talk as being unrealistic generally do so by arguing that 'the government will not permit it to happen.' During the past quarter-century of global prosperity, the idea has taken root that governments know enough about the manipulation of monetary and fiscal policies to prevent serious economic disruptions of the kind experienced in the 1930s. Certainly, as Paul

McCracken explains nearby, they know more now than they did then.

"This thought is comforting, but not that comforting if it merely means that the Federal Reserve will run the money supply to counter every conceivable deflationary pressure that might be arrayed against it. For what Mr. Kahn imagines, a short piece down the road, is a U.S. government faced with choosing between a depression of his definition and an annual inflation rate of 30% or 40%. At some point, he argues, a government will have to pick the depression.

"We see no reason why a future U.S. government has to be faced with that kind of choice. With a nation as educated and, at least at the grass roots, as sensible as ours, there still should be will enough to make the corrections before the collapse, and thus avoid it. The key to this is for policymakers to recognize, as Mr. Kahn does so clearly, that the current fears and risks of depression tomorrow are created by the inflation today. Depression will come only if inflation and inflationary expectations are so high they can be cured no other way.

"In other words, the way to head off depression is to get inflation under control. This in turn means slowing monetary growth. And realistically this cannot be done until monetary policy is freed of the burden of government borrowing and government deficits. So to get the correction under way now, while there is still time to avoid depression, it is clear what must be done."

But what hope can there be that theoreticians and government will keep us from trouble when "Theory Deserts the Forecasters," as *Business Week* discusses in the leading article of its June 29, 1974, issue:

"Economists will remember 1974 for many things: for the squeeze on energy, for the breathtaking rise in prices, and perhaps for events yet to come. But mainly they will remember 1974 as the year the forecasters blew it.

"Passing the midpoint of the year, the forecasters are scrambling to revise the projections they made so bravely last November and December. They disagree not only about the prospects for the economy in 1975 but also about the outlook for the remainder of 1974. They cannot decide whether the U.S. is going into a recession. They cannot even agree on the trend of production, income, and employment at the end of the second quarter."

"As Robert H. Parks, chief economist for Blyth Eastman Dillon Co., says in a footnote to his latest forecast: 'Our caveat is that probability theory (and economic theory) has not been of much help recently. The unprecedented and the dismal seem to come with a regular and stepped-up frequency.' Economists, he concludes, are 'forced to make economic projections more frequently.'

"In other words, even the best forecasts are now out of date shortly after they are constructed.

". . . Economists no longer know what to make of figures that they once thought they could interpret with confidence. The prime statistical series that every forecaster watches for clues to evolving trends have begun to give bewildering signals . . .

"In particular, three great changes have overwhelmed economic theory in recent years:

"° Inflation has become a dominating influence, instead of just an irritating aberration, in practically all the industrialized economies.

"° Serious supply shortages have developed, especially in basic materials.

"° International markets and international money flows often override national economic policies . . ."

"Most economists, however, think there will be no breakthrough in any area of economics. 'There are no signs,' says Samuelson, 'that we're converging toward a philosopher's stone that will cause all the pieces to fall neatly into place.' . . ."

The most frightening aspect of the emerging situation is the spreading fear about the stability of the world's banking system in the West. This is discussed at length in an article on page one of *The Wall Street Journal*, July 26, 1974, signed by Richard F. Janssen:

"Behind the massive stone walls of the Bank of England, the shock waves from the collapse of Germany's Herstatt Bank in late June and the floundering of Franklin National Bank since mid-May are prompting a reorganization of the setup for overseeing London's polyglot financial community, particularly the immense Eurodollar market. There is no pretense of this being a routine reshuffling. It is the first since 1967.

A Strong Wind

"Only straws in the wind. But a strong wind there is, here in the complex of 'Euromarkets' that link all the world's currency and credit markets. Among practitioners and close observers alike, there is just one basic question: Is it a wind that will shake out only the weakest and leave the system itself stronger, or is it an unstoppable whirlwind that will draw the Western world's economies back into the 1930s?

"It may not take very long to find out which is right.

"Within a few weeks, some insiders predict, a number of major banks will have run smack up against their self-set safety limits on how much of their money can be deposited in any other single bank or lent to borrowers in any foreign country. That would pose an unprecedented problem—a few trusted banks having more money than they can lend to qualified borrowers, while at the same time many other banks may be unable to attract deposits they desperately need . . ."

"In its starkest form, the domino theory holds that the collapse of a single sizable bank could weaken many others around the world that had money in it, provoking panicky withdrawals of large deposits that could send them tottering, too. Triggering the initial collapse could be anything from speculative foreign-currency losses to the default of a big borrower, either a government beset by staggering oil-import costs or a corporation caught in an inflationary slump.

" 'The Fed must believe in the domino theory,' surmises one London banker, who reasons that the Federal Reserve otherwise wouldn't have pumped more than $1 billion into Franklin National when other commercial banks suddenly became skittish about providing funds normally. The Bank of England clearly believes that the theory is an all-too-valid one, too, or it wouldn't let it be known that the rescue net is spread and in fact already has been used—even for the less-savory of London's secondary or 'fringe' banks."

This scary situation is again referred to in *The New York Times* column "Market Place" written by Robert Metz, July 31, 1974:

"It is widely known that the drying up of the market for new capital has led corporations to borrow from the nation's banks as never before. As a result, the bank's prime lending rate—the rate charged their most credit-worthy customers—has soared to record levels.

"What is less widely known is that the banks have extended themselves to levels far beyond what the investment community had come to regard as normal.

"While few would suggest that the banking system as a whole is in difficulty, conservative observers both within and outside the banking community are concerned.

"A glance at the critical debt-to-equity ratios of leading banks indicates how dramatically the situation has changed since Congress amended the Bank Holding Company Act in

1970 . . ."

Already, since Mr. Metz wrote the above, several small banks have failed. The gravity of the situation is such that in early September, 1974, representatives of the United States, Switzerland, France, Germany, Italy, Britain, Canada, Sweden, The Netherlands, Belgium and Japan met at Basle to consider the problem of expected bank failures. They failed to reach any common policy for rescuing troubled banks.

All that remains is the *hope* that central banks will bail out any *large* bank that gets into difficulty!

As if the foregoing were not frightening enough, there is additional confirmation of dire forebodings in cycle theory.

One of the first uses of cycle theory is to be found in the Biblical story of Joseph predicting to Pharaoh the seven lean and the seven fat years. It is incontrovertible that the world is subjected to cyclical phenomena—day and night, the phases of the moon and resulting tides, the seasons of the year, and countless others.

A landmark work in the application of Cycle Theory to economic affairs is to be found in *Cycles* by Edward R. Dewey and Edwin F. Dakin of the Foundation for the Study of Cycles, published in 1949, and containing a 1950 postscript. Every serious student of economic forecasting should read and re-read this book. For our purposes here, we will refer only to the discussion in the postscript of the so-called Kondratieff Wave.

Nikolai D. Kondratieff was a professor at the

Agricultural Academy and head of the Business Research Institute of Moscow. After the Russian Revolution, Kondratieff made extensive studies of Western economies which he published between 1922 and 1928. He claimed to have discovered a series of waves in the ups-and-downs of such economies. He discerned a first wave from the end of the 1780s to 1844-1851, which peaked between 1810 and 1817.

A second wave was seen extending from the period between 1844-1851 to 1890-1896, peaking in 1914-1920 when he said the decline seemed to have begun.

This theory clashed with orthodox Marxism which held that capitalism's defects contained the seeds of its own destruction. This wave discovered by Kondratieff indicated the capitalist system was self-correcting. Kondratieff's work was denounced as "wrong and reactionary" and he was banished. In 1930 he was accused of subversive activities, whereupon he was sent to Siberia and oblivion.

Now let us look at the remarkable prediction made by Dewey and Dakin in 1950:

"Who shall date the ending of any Kondratieff so exactly as to say that right here—in 1950, 1952, 1954—the new wave begins to rise? We do know that such a turn is about due; it could even be upon us at this moment; it could be compensating right now for declines in the shorter waves.

"And who can forecast what the new Kondratieff should mean for us in human terms?

Events of today can give us no real clue, even when they now seem important, to the nature of the great creative progress which should accompany the Kondratieff rise—such disparate events as atomic power, steel-making in India, American careers in Arabia, American officers over a Greek army, an electric curtain of radar waves to shield the west from Russia, government controls everywhere to a degree inconceivable even twenty years ago. Who can guess now what is to become really significant for us in the next twenty years?

"From our cyclical data, we can only judge at this moment that we face—as the fifties start —a relatively short time of readjustment; and that afterward the auspices look remarkable. A rising Kondratieff, even without rising trend lines, should be a time of sustained expansion, of growing markets, of new progress in reaching social and industrial goals, of great invention applied in newly creative ways. This new economic springtime should be prevailing for the most of the active life of a whole generation. Bring to it the lift of the simultaneous rises that the fifties should also see in the shorter rhythms, and you begin to sense the dynamic opportunities, the wonderful horizons, that we should be discovering just ahead—as soon as the downward swing, due to reach its nadir in the early fifties, as the main text indicates, has spent itself.

"After the early fifties, as already noted,

there are probabilities that the generation then in its prime may experience no catastrophic depression in its working lifetime —much as this country (despite brief intervening flurries) almost forgot what real industrial depression meant between 1898 and 1929.

"Such are the general outlines of the perspective. Despite all our knowledge, despite all our new tools for judging economic probabilities, we still cannot date the economic turns too exactly, or forecast the amplitude of the waves with accuracy; and we have no exact knowledge that throws really helpful light on the possibilities of another war.

"It remains that we now stand very near a time, considering what probabilities we know, of vast new progress and world reconstruction on a scale quite new to recent American experience. Barring war's cataclysm, those young Americans beginning careers today should find opportunities never even glimpsed by those in the twenties and thirties who called themselves the 'lost' generation. We may well be moving into our nation's greatest years."

In 1972 a study of the Kondratieff Wave in the light of today's developments was made in a book *The Kondratieff Wave* by James B. Shuman and David Rosenau. Geoffrey Barraclough, the British historian reviewing this book, along with eight

—producing major sociological and political changes, including in the phase of downturn 'a strong shift to political conservatism.'

"Finally, if we accept the Kondratieff cycle, it conveys the frightening warning that we are only at the beginning of the 'lean years' and that we must suppose that things will get worse before they get better. To that extent the parallels often drawn between 1971 and 1931 are misleading, and so is the conclusion that as things did not turn out as bad when the dollar went off gold as they did when the pound went off gold in 1931, we are out of the woods. On the contrary, the parallel, if there is one, of 1971 is with 1921, when the boom which began in 1896 ran out, and our comparative place in the cycle today is 1924, not 1934. Evidently, there is still time, as governments fiddle and inflation grows, for another Hitler—or worse."

How all this relates to the price of gold, is clearly summed up by Ronald Segal, no friend of the capitalist system, in his recently published *The Decline and Fall of the American Dollar:*

"The flounderings and gyrations evident in attempts so far to reform the capitalist monetary order support the view that the governments involved will take the necessary action only when driven to it by the consequences of neglect. Certainly the steps at present being contemplated seem far more likely to pro-

others which take a pessimistic view of current events, under the heading "The End of An Era," in *New York Review of Books*, June 27, 1974, attempts to relate the Kondratieff Wave to our current situation:

"And yet, intelligently used—not, that is to say, as a magic wand opening all doors and disclosing all secrets, but as a practical tool—Kondratieff can help us to perceive and understand many features of the current world situation. For one thing, he forces us to view it in historical perspective, not as the unhappy outcome of a series of historical accidents caused by a glut of foot-loose Eurodollars, the greed of Arab sheiks, the costs of the Vietnam war, or the machinations of overmighty multinational corporations (though all these and other things enter in), but rather as a particular phase in a recurrent phenomenon, which has its parallels in the past. In other words, he directs us back—and this is the second point—to earlier periods of large-scale recession—1871 to 1896, or 1921 to 1940—as landmarks from which to take our bearings.

"Thirdly, he makes us aware that the long wave, though economic in origin, is not merely an economic phenomenon. Rather, as Shuman and Rosenau rightly insist, 'It reflects not only major economic trends . . . but all facets of national life—from prosperity to social unrest to involvement in foreign affairs'

national currencies so as to oppose the rise of inflation, might succeed in providing the system with a firmer monetary foot-hold for the while. But this is precisely what the current disposition of the advanced capitalist states precludes. Their governments are as set against any effectual surrender of sovereignty as they are against any effectual measures to defeat inflation. Their efforts at monetary reform essentially constitute an attempt to cure a disease by feeding it with the virus responsible.

"It may well be that, sooner or later, the system will have recourse to gold, with its monetary price raised substantially; perhaps tenfold, to over $400 an ounce. This is not, to be sure, because a rational economic engagement would require it; but because an irrational engagement, needing to rescue itself, would move to do so within its own irrational terms.

"In these terms, such a step would seem to solve several pressing problems at once. It would make feasible a real restoration of convertibility to the dollar, since the United States gold stock, still by far the largest national holding in the world, would increase in value, at around $400 an ounce, to well over $100 billion, or more than enough to supply gold on demand for the foreign wash of dollars. Indeed, paradoxically, the very assurance of such an exchange would neutralize the

mote the economic crisis of capitalism than prevent it.

"The manufacture of special drawing rights, under that or any other name, as the major international reserve asset promises to intensify inflationary pressures and the flight of confidence from paper money. For either the rights will continue to have their value defined in terms of gold, in which event they will uphold gold's monetary role while losing their credibility as an alternative, convertible asset in proportion to the growth of their own role instead, or their connection to gold will formally be cut, and their value will be denominated in terms of various currencies, in which event their real worth will increasingly be questioned, with the attraction of gold commensurately enhanced. Either way, the issue of special drawing rights in sufficient quantity to serve the purpose of issuing them at all must soon enough display the same impulse and impact as the lavish issue of dollars did previously. Indeed, the undertaking to substitute special drawing rights for dollars as the major monetary asset of the capitalist system would amount to the institutionalized transfer of rampant inflation from the predominant printing presses of the United States to those of a collective leadership.

"Only the establishment of a supranational authority, closely controlling the issue of special drawing rights and their relationship to

"Finally, of course, the usefulness of a return to convertibility of the dollar would be dictated by the form of economic breakdown. If this last was massive deflation, with the collapse of credit, then the commitment to convertibility, at a much higher price for gold, would help restore credit and provide a reinflationary drive. If it was that of runaway inflation, it would help to restore confidence in the currency and provide the basis for a controlled deflationary process.

"But, either way, nothing more self-defeating may be imagined than a return to convertibility alongside the headlong pursuit of prodigal economic policies. The new fixed price of gold, however high, would soon enough come to be regarded as no more than a floor supporting speculation on a further rise, or the commitment to convertibility no more than a prelude to another repudiation.

"Thus, the recourse to gold would have to be accompanied by serious economic reform, not only in the United States and other advanced capitalist societies, but of the capitalist monetary system itself. The United States, or any particular alliance of countries, would need to abandon all thought of an imperial role for essentially national currencies, as counterproductive and incompatible with the development of economic forces in the world. And, above all, measures would have to be

need for it, as the establishment of a new fixed price, likely to last for the foreseeable future, made the dollar once again as good as gold.

"It would go far toward discouraging the flight from paper money, since the repudiation by the United States government of dollar convertibility itself so significantly promoted this flight and the related inflationary pressures.

"It might buy time for dealing with the energy predicament as many major suppliers of fossil fuel, with their traditional attachment to gold, effectively exchanged their supplies for gold at its far higher price.

"It would, at a stroke, provide the Soviet Union, as the world's second largest producer of gold, with much augmented resources to purchase, for its ailing economy, productive industrial equipment and even consumer goods from the advanced capitalist countries, in particular the United States. It would proportionately augment the resources of South Africa, the world's largest producer of gold, with its scarcely less repugnant regime, but this would be unlikely to disturb too much the moral sensibilities of capitalist authorities, whose record of righteousness on the issue of South African racism has been so largely rhetorical.

taken to limit the supremacy of gold at the same time that this supremacy was reestablished. Otherwise, it would all too rapidly give rise to the evils it produced in the earlier era of capitalism: an impulse to the sterile rather than the productive investment of wealth; the commitment of so much capital and labor to a product so much of whose value derives from non-use; a confinement or release of economic energy according to fluctuations in new supplies of the metal from mining or private hoards; and the subservience of social decisions to the despotism of gold flows within the international community."

Chapter XV

Conclusion

In the course of the Jewish Day of Atonement (Yom Kippur) service, it is said that it is written in the Book of Life for the coming year, who shall prosper—who shall not prosper; who shall live—who shall die, but that: Repentance, prayer and charity can avert the fateful decree. If repentance means to change our wrong ways and take a new path; if prayer means devoted attention to our new course, and if charity means acting less selfishly, then perhaps the dreadful future so many see coming can be avoided.

But can we expect the world's leaders to change their views, and to concentrate solely on the common good, and to act in the general interest rather than their own narrow national and self-centered immediate ends? If the answer is no, then it would seem that there is little hope of us averting the impending troubles.

Foreseeing the all but inevitable difficulties ahead, it behooves each individual to consider what he can do to survive.

Survival is largely a matter of economics. The lessons of the past demonstrate that the key to economic survival is gold. Gold seems to be the only insurance policy you can buy.

AUTHOR'S NOTE

THERE ARE MANY COMPANIES AND SECURITIES MENTIONED, REFERRED TO, OR BRIEFLY DESCRIBED IN THIS BOOK. INFORMATION RESPECTING THEM WAS TAKEN FROM SOURCES CONSIDERED RELIABLE BUT IN NO WAY GUARANTEED. MOREOVER, THE DATA CONCERNING ANY INDIVIDUAL ISSUE WAS NECESSARILY PREPARED SOME MONTHS AGO, AND CONSEQUENTLY IS OUTDATED. ACCORDINGLY, IF THE READER IS INTERESTED IN ANY OF THE SECURITIES MENTIONED FOR POSSIBLE PURCHASE, SALE OR RETENTION, IT IS ESSENTIAL THAT HE OR SHE ACQUIRE THE LATEST AND MOST AUTHORITATIVE INFORMATION ABOUT IT BEFORE MAKING ANY INVESTMENT DECISION. THIS INFORMATION SHOULD BE SECURED FROM THE COMPANY OR A RESPONSIBLE BROKER, DEALER, INVESTMENT ADVISOR, FINANCIAL PUBLICATION, OR SERVICE. IN NO EVENT IS ANY RECOMMENDATION OR ENDORSEMENT OF ANY SECURITY MADE OR IMPLIED; AND NOTHING HEREIN IS TO BE CONSIDERED UNDER ANY CIRCUMSTANCES AS AN OFFER OR INDUCEMENT TO BUY, SELL, OR HOLD ANY SECURITY AT ANY TIME.

Chapter XVI

Prospects For The 1980's

So much for the context at the onset of the Eighties. Which direction now?

The first point we would make is one which I have reiterated from $350 an ounce on: the current price is not sustainable, in our opinion. It is so far removed from any "normal" equilibrium that one of two things appear likely to occur, and these would reflect forces that have nothing to do with gold itself.

The first possibility is that the world is indeed in the early stages of profound and prolonged economic and political turmoil. This is the world the gold bugs have always warned about: accelerating inflation, social chaos, war. Under this scenario, $800 an ounce would be a bargain.

The alternative scenario would also be painful but would entail healthier longer-term prospects: disinflation to help wring excesses from the economic fabric of the major countries, reduced *real* energy costs, a redirection of emphasis from consumption to savings and investment, and stemming the worldwide sweep of Russian (as well as Cuban and sundry other surrogate mercenary) troops. If this scenario materializes, bullion could collapse to under $300 an ounce over the months and years ahead.

Which is it to be?

Much as we detest two-handed economists, we must conclude that we don't know. Each investor must make his own subjective value judgment as to the likely outcome of events. *In this sense, gold merely mirrors the collectively-perceived prospective erosion in purchasing power.*

Our own assessment for 1980 includes the following assumptions:

Supplies will show a marked decline. We strongly doubt that the IMF will initiate a new selling program after expiration of the present 425,000 ounce-a-month one expires in May. Further, pressure is growing on the U.S. Treasury to moderate or suspend its sales, the mirage of demonetization having so obviously evaporated. South African supplies will decline in light of the higher prices. On the other hand, we expect a small increase in other free world supplies for the same reason. Finally, we look for considerably larger sales by Russia, now that U.S. banks and corporations may not fall over each other quite so readily to shore up its inefficient economy with food, goods, and above all credits.

We expect the two most significant aspects of demand in 1980 to be a very steep decline in jewelry, and another jump in investment demand.

The reasons for expecting lower jewelry demand are obvious, given the price sensitivity in the developing world and the Middle East, and the effect of decelerating economic growth in the OECD countries on disposable incomes. Our fairly high figures for coin and investment demand partly reflect our expectation that the level of inflation will remain high even if and as economic growth decelerates worldwide. It also partly reflects another and potentially much more unsettling factor: *The ballooning OPEC surpluses in search of safe havens.*

I have often reminded our clients that the distinction between public and private funds, as well as between official, semi-official, and private institutions, is by no means as clear-cut in the Middle East (or, for that matter, in Japan) as it is in the U.S. Timothy Green, consultant to Consolidated Gold Fields, has pointed out that total gold official reserves in the Middle East amount to a mere 1,300 metric tons. This is less than in Belgium or Switzerland, and compares with 8,000 tons in the U.S., 3,500 tons in France and 3,700 tons in Germany. Yet an OPEC surplus of $50 billion is enough to purchase twice the amount of all new gold coming on the market at $400 an ounce. Even that incredible statistic does not take into account OPEC government investment authorities, or the fact that OPEC's surpluses may approach $80-100 billion in 1980.

D. Potential Price Pitfalls

Some of the implications are so negative that

the commonsense urge for survival dictates that they are unthinkable for all parties concerned. In fact, it would be irresponsible for each fiduciary or individual not to at least recognize and assess the prospects of the various forces which, if they materialized, would in all likelihood bring about a sharp drop in the gold price.

Our list would include the following. Please note that none of the items below necessarily involves approval or disapproval. Rather, each is presented as the sort of event which, if it occurred, could be expected to bring about a significant change in collective perception and involve a reduction in the comparative attraction of holding gold relative to financial assets:

1. Sharp and prolonged economic slowdown, which would reduce the rate of inflation, and increase returns on financial assets.
2. Profit-taking, with price changes accentuated by an absence of buyers, just as the closing months of 1979 were characterized by an absence of sellers.
3. Wage, price, credit, and exchange controls.
4. An improved balance of trade and payments.
5. A strong Carter reaction to the Russian invasion of Afghanistan, bringing about a halt to Russian/Cuban/mercenary aggression in the Middle East, Africa, Southeast Asia, and the Caribbean.
6. Prospects for the election of a strong Republican successor who would so act.

7. Concerned central bank moves to cool the precious metals markets, in view of the worldwide inflationary implications of the rise in bullion prices.

Again, there can be no definitive answers to these questions; each individual must provide his own assessment and interpretation.

Biography of James E. Cavallo

Jim Cavallo was born in 1949 and grew up in a small suburb of New York. He attended Pace University majoring in Taxation & Accounting. After founding and operating his own insurance agency catering to small businesses, he joined Shearson Loeb Rhoades as Senior Financial Consultant. He has also been a personal financial consultant to many magazine publishers and has lectured in many financial districts across the U.S.

Now with DBL in New York City as Vice President of Financial Services, and in this capacity deals in diversified investment counseling.

Now with Drexel, Burnham Lambert in New York City as Vice President of Financial Services, and in this capacity deals in diversified investment counseling.

Mr. Cavallo is now with Drexel, Burnham Lambert in New York City as Vice President of Financial Services, and in this capacity deals in diversified investment counselling.